Preface

Table of Contents

CHAPTER 3 : THE SHOCK

CHAPTER 4 : THE EXCHANGE

CONCLUSION

THE WORLD IS YOUR CLASSROOM

Everyone says that doing an exchange, studying abroad will change your life. You pack your bags with high expectations because you've already heard so much about it that you expect something big. You prepare your journey to make the most out of it so that you don't lose a second of this experience. But the truth is, no one can prepare you for this.

There's no other experience like it in life. It's a roller coaster of emotions and new experiences, cultural shock, fear, wonderment, openness, learning, acceptance, surprise, discovery, exploration, love, happiness, heartbreak, homesickness, sadness, gratitude, euphoria, and compassion. On this roller coaster, you'll experience all of these ups and downs, but in the end, the only feeling you won't experience is regret. No one regrets this leap of faith. At the end of your Erasmus journey, you'll become stronger, smarter, and more flexible, passionate and tenacious. You'll become an action taker.

Coming home, you'll no longer be the person you were when you first packed your bags. This adventure would have changed who you are. Exchange isn't a year in your life; it's life in a year. Erasmus one day, Erasmus forever.

For me, the meaning of life is to have as many outside-of-your-comfort-zone experiences on this earth as possible to build my body, mind, and soul into the best versions they can be. That way, I can then make a significant impact on this world. At this point, from my wild journey, there's no other experience that serves as strong that purpose as going to my first exchange in Milan in 2010. It was an experience that radically switched me to a better path and became the foundation of my newfound lifestyle—it made me reflect and retrospect; I was able to look deeper within myself.

As hard as it may sound, my exchange in Milan was literally the beginning of my life. Before that point, I was mostly daydreaming, naive, unconscious, and staying mostly in my comfort zone. To top it off, I had even received the "dreamer award" at my high school diploma ceremony. That first massive jump into the unknown led me into a lifestyle of taking action. That decision led me to building a million-dollar business, traveling to more than 40 countries, living in more than five of them, and jumping on all immersive experiences that could bring me to the next level.

Like most of you, it was my first time outside my parents' home, my first time living in a flatshare, first time buying my grocery and cleaning the house, first time taking a plane, and first time traveling and doing a road trip of more than five days. Just like you, it was a series of firsts for me, but it was also my first time connecting so deeply with other human beings, my first time living the community lifestyle. How hard it would have been for our parents to go abroad for one semester back then. Now, the university exchange student experience has been made famous around the world through the renowned successful Erasmus Program, highly acclaimed movie, *L'auberge Espagnole*, and the last 40–50+ years of worldwide university partnerships growing their networks year after year. How lucky we are to live in this moment in time where it is so easy to press a button to leave and go explore; you would be foolish not to jump into this opportunity.

The world is your classroom; you won't learn much from your textbooks following the normal university degree path. You need to push yourself and use every opportunity the university social life has to give you. Going abroad for one semester is by far the most underrated offering of the university journey. The hidden truth that no one talks about the study-abroad experience is that it makes you escape from the daily local news, TV, sports fans' general conversations, gossip about other people, etc. and all the habits that keep you hooked into a routine comfort lifestyle.

Constantly pushing yourself outside of your comfort zone is the key to life. You can start by taking a first flight overseas that will lead you to presenting yourself to strangers, trying new things you have never done and never heard of, jumping on random adventures, starting bold projects, and going on intense immersive retreats. This is the way to grow and all the best memories of your life will be linked to these moments.

So tell me...Do you think you have enough information about what you are about to live? Do you have enough support as you do this big jump? Did you learn from the past experiences of others?

I hope you are ready because I'm bringing you along for a ride filled with deep emotional flips, spiritual sharp turns, and a self-growth journey of ups and downs leading you to so many eye-opening contents and concepts toward your best version.

I'm proud of you! By taking this book, you have gone a long way already.

I love you so much. You are part of my family now.

Your new life has just begun.

"THE WORLD IS A BOOK AND THOSE WHO DO NOT TRAVEL READ ONLY ONE PAGE."

~ SAINT AUGUSTINE

HOW I MET ERASMUS

I could have joined the most public university in Montreal that gave the right to education to everyone over 21 years old because my grades were not good enough to be accepted in private institutions. That was a defining moment for me, and it was when I committed to flipping my life around and making a man of myself. I had taken a strong commitment to putting a stop to all bad relationships and habits I had for years. I knew deep inside that there was more out there for me.

I was so excited about this new life that I went to join the official visit to the university a few days before the classes started. This is the kind of event that not many people go to, but I decided to go in the hopes of making new friends. Although I didn't meet anyone that day, it definitely changed my life forever.

After the university visit, the dean gave the usual welcome speech in the big auditorium and then went on to welcome the president of the biggest student association. WOW, this guy was something else - charming, loud, extroverted, popular, and funny. He brought amazing energy in there that you wanted to be that guy on that stage at that very moment. His whole ecstatic speech was all about how he just lived the best three years of his life in that university jumping on all the social and outside-class opportunities. From events to business challenges; from volunteering to being the president of one of the main associations.

Of all the things he had amazingly done, however, he shared that the only thing he regretted is not going on a semester abroad to do a student exchange. The way he said it, I got hooked. I didn't know what a student exchange was at that time, but I knew I needed to do that. It was THE thing I was searching for to flip my life around. A brand new start.

MY FIRST ERASMUS IN MILAN

One and a half years passed from the moment I heard the eye-opening speech to the time I left for my first exchange in Milan. Like a real lost young man expert procrastinator, I didn't prepare or even research much before arriving in Europe for the first time. It was on a cold Canadian winter day that my mom drove me to the airport for the first time. With a brand new 23kg luggage and pocket digital camera, I walked through the airport trying to find my way towards my check-in gate. I was so lost; I was like a kid going out of the house for the first time. Each time I look at my video and photo souvenirs of that time, I cry of nostalgia.

It was 2010, things were very different back then; smartphones were not affordable and airport free wifi was not accessible. I was terrified of that first flight; like most of us, I got traumatized by the idea of the plane crash in the ocean and having no control over it. I was also terrified of my arrival. *What if I get lost? What if I get robbed?* Thank God, I had a contact to host me for the first few days to explain the principles to get by. I don't know what I would have done without her. But, hey, guess what, even with her support, I got lost on my way towards her house. No phone numbers and no Google map app, I had no choice but to ask for help in the street like the good old days where humans needed to talk to each other. I was beyond myself when I realized at that moment that barely anyone was speaking English. I thought, "I'm in big trouble". But after asking a few people, I found this cute couple who could speak English and they helped me get to my destination.

Not many people were speaking English at that time, and each time I met a local, they thought I was an extraterrestrial. That made it harder for me than I thought, but in a sense, it made the experience even more charming and equally challenging.

Over time, I learned to embrace that fact and jump in deep on exploring that incredible culture that made this "Dolce Vita" that people keep dreaming of. The wood-oven fresh pizza, homemade pasta, juicy Buffalo mozzarella, ancient Roman ruins, wine valley of Tuscany, the cute Vespas turning the street corners, the Leonardo Da Vinci or Michelangelo art, the handmade supercars: Ferrari and Lamborghini, the world-famous hand gesture when they talk, the famous football clubs, the irresistible gelato, without forgetting their world-famous sights like the Tower of Pisa, the Rome Colosseum, the Pantheon, the Trevi Fountain, the Vatican, the Milan Duomo, the Grand Canal of Venice, the Opera of Verona, Lake Como, the Amalfi Coast, the Cinque Terre, etc. Italy will forever be my second home.

Today, I say playfully that my heart is in Thailand, my mouth is in Italy, my mind is in Canada, and my hips are in Colombia.

"YOU MAY HAVE THE UNIVERSE IF I MAY HAVE ITALY."

~ GIUSEPPE VERDI, ITALIAN COMPOSER

SELLING THE ERASMUS DREAM

Promoting the exchange student experience has been my vocation since I returned from Milan in 2010. I had jumped on my first semester abroad in Milan with a hunger to switch my life around. I had never been happier before than I was at this point in my life because my eyes were in constant discovery mode of every little thing around me. I was constantly pushing myself out of my comfort zone, discovering the world, experiencing new cultures, and discovering myself. I came back home a new man trying to convince everyone I encounter to jump into this life-changing journey and helping my university ESG UQAM (École des Sciences de la Gestion) international student desk to promote the student exchange experience while pitching my story from class to class. Seeing people's eyes glow, how attentive and fascinated they were during my presentations, really inspired me. It pushed me to continue. I thought that people only needed a little motivation, so I started selling the dream to everyone I knew.

During this period of my life, I was invited to the office of a senior administrator of my university in order to thank me for my involvement. It was during this friendly conversation that I had a flash, the kind of flash that changes your life forever. We were talking about how great it is to do a semester abroad in Europe, with all the associations and organizations uniquely organized for exchange students. And, together, we asked ourselves why there isn't an organization like that in Montreal or not even a simple student association at my university. The reaction I got from her when I asked that question got me thinking so deep at that moment. It was then that I knew I wanted to create an organization that will change the exchange student experience coming to Montreal.

From this point, I started months of research, market studies, and business plan creation. That's it, I finally found my career path.

"I BELIEVE THAT EVERYTHING IS POSSIBLE, I SEE OPPORTUNITY WHERE OTHERS SEE IMPOSSIBILITY, I TAKE RISKS, I AM FOCUSED, I HUSTLE, I FEEL OVERWHELMING LOVE. I EMBRACE MY CHILDLIKE WONDER AND CURIOSITY. I TAKE FLYING LEAPS INTO THE UNKNOWN, I CONTRIBUTE TO SOMETHING BIGGER THAN MYSELF, I CREATE, I LEARN, I GROW, I DO. I BELIEVE IT IS NEVER TOO LATE TO START LIVING A DREAM, I AM AN ENTREPRENEUR."

~ ANONYMOUS

After this semester in Montreal, I left for the second exchange in Paris. Well, it was in Évry, 45 minutes south Paris, at Telecom SudParis. I made my registration at the beginning of my exchange in Milan when I realized that it was the best decision I had ever made in my life. Things had been a lot different during this second time while missing the special organization satisfying the social life of exchange students and living in a close university campus far from the city center.

This experience confirmed my business idea of creating an organization only for exchange students in Montreal. I analyzed everything and saw all the little things the exchange students were missing out from the first experience. But I still managed to make the most of it while visiting other countries, my friends from my Milan exchange, and living the unique France student social life organized by the main student club of the school.

One thing I really took advantage of was the immersive one-week entrepreneurial business case where the whole school is free from classes and students are asked to build in-depth business plans while attending workshops on the art of creating a business. I managed to ask some friends to do it on InterStude, which helped me a lot with clarifying my ideas. It was the start of my entrepreneurial journey.

After that semester in Paris, I received my bachelor's degree diploma, went back to Montreal for the summer, did more market research, found a business partner, and launched some free cultural events for the new incoming exchange students of the fall semester of 2011.

INTERSTUDE,
MY LIFE,
MY BUSINESS

I was obsessed with making it, to become a successful man. Since I finished my bachelor's degree in 2011, I've dedicated 100% of my life to InterStude and my dream to help Montreal by making it the best destination to do an exchange abroad. InterStude is an organization satisfying the social life of young international students staying temporarily in Montreal offering bus trips, cultural events, parties, community infrastructure, and educative content.

What gave birth to InterStude is my desire to live out of the nine-to-five corporate lifestyle. I wanted to live another Erasmus experience over and over again while connecting with like-minded people from all around the world and enriching my life with meaningful travel experiences. Building a community in this niche was the best way I found to support this vision.

With zero professional experience, this organization poured on me a lot of challenges. But looking back, the first three years of the journey were the most blissful time of my life. I was traveling every weekend, leading tours, pushing the creative boundaries on creating new and unique trips, meeting thousands of global citizens, and connecting with so many people at a deeper level. Over the years, we traveled with more than 15000 international students through more than 300 buses traveling around 25 North American destinations.

But I didn't reach that success alone. InterStude came a long way over the years with the help of more than 100 employees, volunteers, freelancers, tour leaders, and interns. What started from a simple desire to travel and perpetuate the life-changing exchange I had in Milan, InterStude evolved and grew to promote a lifestyle a lot of young people wanted to connect with. This niche community, combined with good branding of coolness factor, made several people want to be part of this experience of bringing InterStude to the top.

It was another roller-coaster journey, but every piece of it was worth it, even if many times it drove me crazy that I just wanted to quit. I realized that the journey itself was happiness with all its imperfections - traveling in groups, discovering all those new cities, changing the lives of thousands of international students, growing personally and spiritually, living with all those deep roller-coaster emotions, connecting deeply with some fellow coworkers, and learning so much about the business world, myself, and the universe.

All of it was priceless. Like it was discovered through a Harvard study involving 5000 people from different backgrounds and society levels, three things are responsible for making people happy: living in a community, close relationship with deep communication with our core family and, lastly, strong life partner relation.[1]

Here's my best advice: go on and build your own community on a topic you connect with other people. Create a free Facebook event or a monthly Meetup and don't give up. In the beginning, one or two persons will show up. Slowly, you'll learn how to improve it and you'll learn about your communities' needs on top of building many skills. And who knows maybe one day it can become a non-profit or business or just a place where you feel deeply at home meeting your best friends, your second family.

Building your community is the best way to satisfy all your life dimensions while constantly growing into the best version of yourself.

---

[1] https://news.harvard.edu/gazette/story/2017/04/over-nearly-80-years-harvard-study-has-been-showing-how-to-live-a-healthy-and-happy-life/

HOW TO USE THIS BOOK

This book is my gift to the Erasmus and university exchange student market. It's nine years of experience and knowledge on this topic that I'm sharing together with my love and advocacy for self-development. This book is a compass that will help you to navigate correctly through every stage of your Erasmus. It has been created so that you can venture into this temporary but life-changing experience to discover yourself deeply and start visualizing a magical life all while becoming your best version.

Every big period of the experience has been separated chronologically into a chapter. Most subsections have checklist action plans, some of my personal stories on the subject, and also exchange students' stories I've picked up over the years. Each chapter has at least one case study giving you clear examples and an interview with experts in the industry.

To make the most of this book, I highly recommend you to stop reading when there are exercises and actually do them in your notebook or journal. Don't expect to continue reading and come back on it later; it won't happen.

Finally, all the appendices are extra content to maximize your self-growth after your Erasmus.

Enjoy the journey!

You are the master of your life.

CHAPTER 1:

The Dream

AMAZED AT THE OPPORTUNITY TO LIVE THE EXPERIENCE OF YOUR LIFE

1 - HEARING ABOUT 'THE EXPERIENCE'
Excitement rushes in and the dream begins

This situation has definitely happened to you already. You met someone who lived the experience and he sold you his dreamed experience. His enthusiasm for this experience probably surprised you and it pushes you to learn more about the subject.

From the moment you hear about it the first time, you are either hooked, like me, or not. At this point, I'm guessing you are hooked. From that point, you set an intention to the universe and you'll hear about the experience everywhere you go. After my awakening day listening to that association president's speech, I randomly stumbled on a guy promoting his experience in the hallway of the university.

Then one day, a girl randomly showed up to my class to present her journey with a beautiful diaporama of kickass photos of her experience. She was so ecstatic talking about her experience. She got all my attention, but somehow I realized I was one of a few people interested. It felt so strange to me that people wouldn't be interested in this magical opportunity. A question I asked myself for a long time until I realized the answer is the same reason why people always stay in their comfort zone telling themselves white lies.

White lies are those tiny self-thoughts you autosuggest of reasons about why you are doing one thing or not doing another thing. A self-rational explanation validating your behavior. Like I watch sports because I like the fan emotions of it, but never admitting the fact that the majority of people have been sold on it by advertisers' mind tricks and the rest of the people are just unconscious followers doing what other people are doing to fit in. But why do people like to stay in their comfort zone? They simply don't take many chances with their life because of deep inner fears of rejection, being judged, failure, death, lack of belief in themselves, or being scared of the struggles.

INSPIRATION

Here are 3 YouTube videos that sell you or anyone to jump on this life-changing adventure. By watching those videos, you'll feel a sense of envy making you even more excited about it:

1. Exchange Your Life Book Trailer for Kickstarter // Erasmus Students

2. Welcome to Erasmus - if Erasmus Had a Trailer

3. #THISisESN - the Erasmus Student Network

2 - HOW TO MANIFEST YOUR DREAMS
Everything you wish is possible

I have always been inspired by the idea of the Law of Attraction ever since I was a teenager and first watched the documentary, 'The Secret'. The Law of Attraction is a universal principle that is already working in your life. Start intentionally thinking and feeling what it is you want to attract into your life — such as money, love and relationships, health and spirituality, etc. — to make the Law of Attraction work for you. When the documentary came out, it was very controversial because the non-believers were outraged by the way it was presented as an effortless thing to just think, visualize and it will come to you by magic.

Obviously, the documentary was made in a marketing sense to be pushy and controversial, to encourage mass talk about it. That's the beauty of hidden marketing pushing the word to mouth. But you need to step back from the straight-to-point claims and analyze the concept in depth.

Having a vision for your life is the only way to move forward. Sometimes vision is not well put in place from a lack of understanding of yourself, conditionings, and subconscious patterns. But it doesn't matter much at this point because the vision will make you take action, give the excitement to move forward and grow that over time you'll realize some other truths.

There are many ways to visualize your future:
- **A vision board like in 'The Secret.'** Pin images from the web or magazines on a pin board you keep your room.
- **A small pocket notebook.** Split it into sections, and for each page, put an image of a desire with a date to attain it.
- **A laptop or phone wallpaper.** Use Canva.com to create a funky collage of your top two vision photos of each wheel of life dimensions.

- **A written essay in the present tense.** Like from the 'Become Your Best Version' workbook resume in the appendix, analyze yourself deeply to then write an extremely detailed three-year vision in the present tense.
- **Creative meditation techniques.** Every morning during your meditation, visualize the things you want and feel them as if they are already happening.

Your thoughts create your reality. This is best demonstrated by the rice experiment of Dr. Masaru Emoto where he put rice in three different jars and labeled the jar: Love, Hate, Ignore.

Over a period of two months, you focus on positive energy praising the 'Love' one, you say negative things to the 'Hate' one and you don't look at the 'Ignore' one. The 'Love' one ends up in perfect shape, the 'Hate' one is ultra-dark and contaminated with mushrooms, and the 'Ignore' one is mid-way contaminated and moist.

Even more incredible is that he conducted a similar experience where the subject directs a certain emotion to water to come to the results that water captures emotions and turns into ice crystals under a highly magnified photograph. More studies have shown that water, not only has memory, but also its structure is affected by the emotions of people when interacting with positive or negative emotions.

So realizing your dreams is a matter of thought monitoring. We have between 50, 000 to 70, 000 thoughts a day, which needs a high level of awareness, living mindfully every moment, being aware of the negative thoughts and bad frequencies. The practice of meditation enhances this awareness over time. After 200+ hours of practice, you should start seeing some results. Also, what is highly beneficial is to keep a personal journal where you note every subconscious reaction that is worth analyzing. Once you are aware of your patterns, then you have tools to understand how your subconscious works.

The trick to keep the positive thoughts flowing throughout the day is to set an intention for the day and for specific events of the day. Then obviously have a balanced day fulfilling all your seven life dimensions, but also keeping your willpower to high levels with positive thoughts, praising actions, sunbath, meditation, healthy eating, and physical activities.

Affirmation and autosuggestion are also extremely important. The goal is to control your self-talks; your inner conversation with yourself and the mind. This millions of years old mind that is a program to make you survive in the wild has a lot of auto protective settings helping you and sometimes not so. I AM affirmation of what you want to be, act, work on, are the best and easiest way to go. Repeat them constantly from the moment you wake up to when you have one minute of spare time waiting in line. Monk uses bracelets of 108 beans, touching them one after the other while reciting their mantra similar to affirmation.

A great aspiration dream gives you the excitement feeling pushing you out of bed in the morning. The closest thing to happiness is excitement. Excitement is a mixture of enthusiasm, motivation, intuition, and a hint of creativity giving you the faith you need to feel you'll accomplish what you want.

3 - HOW TO GO OUT OF YOUR COMFORT ZONE
It will lead you to your best memories

Understand that, number one, your brain is busy processing all the subconscious tasks in order to make you function every second of every day. Number two, your brain is lazy, because it needs so much energy to process everything that it doesn't want to do something more and challenging. Third, your brain wants to keep you safe, as that is a survival mechanism that was equipped in us humans millions of years ago when we needed to survive in the wild. So, change is hard because you are wired to expect the worst.

But why is it primordial to learn to get out of your comfort zone? Because...

- The best things happen outside of your comfort zone.
- It will help you create the best memories.
- To use it to learn about you and the universe.
- You'll be more productive.
- You'll have an easier time dealing with new and unexpected changes.
- To grow. Like a muscle, you need to stretch it to its limit so that it can then grow.
- To become more mindful and aware of life's little things.
- To learn to take risks. You'll need it to achieve your big dreams.

What is something that you've been putting off because it brings butterflies to your stomach? Is there a slight fear you have? The energy of your fears literally stays stuck in your kidneys when not confronted. Use *the 5 Second Rule* by Mel Robbins to get yourself out of your comfort zone in the present moment. Once you sense your brain hesitating to take an action you wish you could take now, start counting backward 5-4-3-2-1 and jump. It tricks the prefrontal cortex of your brain, the part used for rational thinking. Once the hesitation sets in, the automatic response of the brain is to stop you from acting because it wants to keep you safe.

Watch on YouTube this incredible interview: *Mel Robbins on Why Motivation Is Garbage | Impact Theory*

Here's a list of things that are outside of the comfort zone of most people:

- Dancing or/and singing in public.
- Being in front of a camera.
- Telling your parents "I LOVE YOU" and hugging them with your head on the right side for a heart-to-heart connection.
- Saying "YES" to something that you normally wouldn't consider.
- Starting a conversation with strangers.
- Asking a question putting people off-guard.
- Taking a cold shower.
- Giving up control.
- Cold calling to sell something on the phone.
- Eating insects or the most disgusting foreign food.
- Facing your fear of heights! With bungee, skydiving, and paragliding.
- Being a naked model for a painting or photo shoot sessions.
- Giving a public speaking presentation in front of 50+ people.
- Visiting a country that its culture is the complete opposite of yours.
- Going on an immersive experience of more than 10 days while pausing your life.
- Asking someone on a date who you think is way out of your league.
- Having a fierce conversation with a person you wish you had for a long time.
- Taking a homeless person out to lunch and hearing their story.
- Going on a water fast for three days and intaking nothing but water.

Steps to get out of your comfort zone:

- List all your fears and what makes you uncomfortable.
- Have a plan and hold yourself accountable.
- Trust yourself and make fast decisions.
- Do it in small steps. Think of a mountain climber; when they begin climbing mountains, they don't start with Everest. They start with smaller peaks until they build up a tolerance.
- Take three deep breaths. Think of something that brings you great joy. Picture your whole body filling up with a bright glow, like a light bulb, as you think of your great joy.
- Find yourself an accountability partner.

We may not be aware of how comfortable we are in our comfort zone. The more we take risks in the right ways, the more we reach our next level. Within years, we will be amazed by what we have become and achieved. Never give up, keep striving for the next level of your best version. Life is a beautiful playground to free yourself from your mind and connect with your inner soul.

4 - INTENSIVE RESEARCH ON ALL POSSIBILITIES
Exploring a whole new world

So you slowly start to inform yourself on the subject by starting with the internet of course. You flip through the school's website to see the different admission requirements and then explore the different destinations offered by your university.

After my little research on the web, I decided to take a little visit to the international student's office. I was frankly impressed to meet remarkable people. I noticed that everyone who worked there were past exchange students all having the light. They all had an experience that changed their lives forever and decided to give back to society by supporting students' leave to experience the world.

That's where I discovered this little hidden world and understood the real definition of the phrase that you will surely hear many times, "Erasmus one day, Erasmus forever". Returning from your experience, you will see, meet someone who has lived the experience and you'll connect for a thrilling conversation of several hours.

After visiting the international office of your school, I suggest you attend one of the conferences or workshops they offer to inform you in-depth on the subject. It also helps you to meet students who have lived the experience to ask them all the questions that go through your head. Also, it is a good opportunity to meet future exchange students like you.

CHECKLIST FOR YOUR RESEARCH STAGE:

- ☐ Visit the international section of your school website and more precisely the exchange student program.

- ☐ Read the registration form to see all the requirements.

- ☐ Explore the different partner universities of your university.

- ☐ Meet a counselor at the international students' desk at your school.

- ☐ Attend an information conference or workshop offered by the international students' desk.

- ☐ Attend other events offered by the international students' desk, sample cocktail gathering "Ex-Erasmus" and "Future-Erasmus".

- ☐ Choose your top ten countries you want to experience their culture.

- ☐ Choose your top ten universities you wish you could live on their campus life.

- ☐ Find yourself a blog of a student who has gone to your wanted destination and read all their adventures.

- ☐ Ask your international students' desk counselor to put you in contact with students that have gone to the destinations you want to go.

- ☐ Always try to go with your intuition gut feeling, the first 45 seconds psyche reaction.

- ☐ Combine your top countries with top universities to create your top three application choices.

5 - EXPLORE YOURSELF BEFORE EXPLORING THE WORLD
You take the best decision when you know yourself deeply

The best way to know yourself deeply is to sit down and do the work. In will take you around eight hours to go over the entire 'Become Your Best Version' workbook that is summarized in the Appendix.

Right now, let's start with the base, the most common personality test, the MBTI. You can do it in 12 minutes for free on this extremely informative and user-friendly website, 16personalities. com. Save your results for future users; your personality may change over a two-year period depending on your life experiences. Then read the nine pages of content of your results about how you see the world.

Yes, there are only 16 players to play this game of life, so if you want to maximize the game, you better know well what you are playing with.

HERE ARE 70 LIFE QUESTIONS THAT WILL GET YOU STARTED ON YOUR SELF-EXPLORATION:

1. Describe yourself in three adjectives.
2. What are the things that make you the most happy?
3. Who is the person that makes you the most happy?
4. What is the thing you did last year that made you the most happy?
5. What do you LOVE (in your personal and professional life, the contrary of what you hate)?
6. What are you GOOD AT (that you might like or not like to do)?
7. What does the WORLD NEED (from your own perspective & vision of the world)?
8. What can you get PAID FOR (the skills you bring on the table to grow your organization or team)?
9. What you don't like to do in your personal and professional life.
10. List your top ten values you live with or would like to live by.
11. What are all the emotions you lived last week, what happened and why (negative emotions are patterns that need to be broken)?
12. What are your fears? Ask yourself, 'What if I...(list your fear happening)?' Really ask yourself why you are feeling that way to arrive at the bottom core.
13. What are all your resources (knowledge, contacts, skills, colleagues, assets, experiences, material, etc.)
14. What are you most grateful for in your life?
15. What drives you?
16. What did you like to do when you were a child?
17. What are your top three favorites movies and why?
18. What are your top three favorites books and why?
19. What are your passions?

20. Are you more of a beach/water person or mountain/forest?
21. What conference, convention, exposition would you like to go and why?
22. If you would have an extra $1000 to spend, what would you do with it?
23. What are your favorite characters from movies, novels, TV series?
24. Who are your models and inspirations?
25. What is your reason to wake up, your ikigai, your purpose?
26. What do you need to let go of?
27. What is your biggest dream?
28. What's the nicest thing you've ever done?
29. What is your earliest memory of love?
30. What has been the most challenging situation so far in your life?
31. What's your greatest accomplishment?
32. What's the best advice you ever got?
33. When you think of successful, who's the first person that comes to mind?
34. What are your daily habits and routines?
35. What would the best day of your life look like?
36. Just before you die, what are the three truths that you could pass on to the people you love?
37. What would you say right now to your 80-year-old self?
38. What are the three books you would leave behind to your loved ones?
39. What are you looking for in a friendship?
40. How would the world become better as a result of your impact? What is your legacy?
41. What activity in your life lights you up with joy?
42. What have you done in your life that you are most proud of?
43. If you could have one wish granted, what would it be?
44. What are your highest core values?

45. How comfortable are you with your own mortality?
46. Who is the most important person in your life?
47. How do you feel about your parents?
48. How is your relationship with money?
49. To your best knowledge, how do other people perceive you?
50. What do you believe is the meaning of your life?
51. What's one thing you would like to do more of and why? How can you make that happen?
52. What's one thing you would like to do less of and why? How can you make that happen?
53. What would you like to stop worrying about? What steps can you take to let go of the worry?
54. When you're in physical or emotional pain, what are some of the best things you can do for yourself?
55. Do you have unfinished business? With whom? What inner work needs to be done to heal this? What steps can you take to bring resolution?
56. How do you sabotage yourself?
57. How do you feel about your relationship with your body?
58. What makes you feel most like yourself. Why?
59. Are you getting too caught up in other people's problems?
60. What is your happiest memory?
61. Are there areas of your life that you notice you compare yourself to others? Your body, your job, etc.
62. What do you want people to say about you at your funeral?
63. How do you feel and react when you fail?
64. Do you quickly get defended or cut off to avoid uncomfortable/negative thoughts or emotions? Which emotions? Why do you think you do this?
65. If you had one year to live, what would you try to achieve?
66. What good habits do you want to cultivate?
67. When did you last push the boundaries of your comfort zone? Do you avoid doing this? When? Why?

68. What emotion do you often tap into and is most familiar to you (e.g., worry, anger, frustration, etc.)? If you were to look more in-depth and beneath that feeling, what might you find (e.g., sadness, disappointment, etc.)? Are you willing to go there? Why or why not?

69. Who has had the greatest impact on your life? Why? In what way?

70. Are there times you feel like giving up? What leads you to that state?

6 - HOW TO CHOOSE THE RIGHT DESTINATIONS?
The biggest decision of your life

This step is crucial, a life-changing decision. If you do not know yet, you must choose your top three host universities to apply.

First, the choice of destinations will depend on your domain of studies. You have the advantage of choosing a school that specializes in your field of study. Moreover, it is extremely important to check the equivalent courses that you can find internationally. People in accounting usually have trouble finding equivalent courses.

Secondly, the choice will depend on your personality and experience. If you have traveled to Europe before, I suggest you go for a more adventurous choice like Asia or South America. You must first choose a continent that challenges you, then a country that the culture fascinates you, and finally, a dynamic city full of social and cultural offerings. Also, make sure your host university has a very dynamic and modern campus with all kinds of social life offerings.

Thirdly, you must take into account in your researches what is offered to exchange students in the city you think you want to go to. Does the host university have an active international students' office with access to several resources? Does the university have at least 250 students in exchange for each semester? Is there an association for exchange students or an organization in the city offering trips and events exclusively to exchange students? Leaving the best exchange is all about having this strong and diverse community of exchange students from around the world.

Here are some suggestions for finding answers to these questions. Search groups or pages on Facebook. For example, "exchange students to...", "Erasmus...". Do your research in English and also in the language of the country. Also, do these keyword searches on Google; you might have better luck. Finally, ask any student you can find on the web who has already lived the experience in the university you want to go to.

On top of all of the above, you should also take into consideration the student's visa needed, how hard it is to learn the basics of the language, and the destinations to visit outside of your host city.

Here are pros and cons per continent to decide what you are looking for:

EUROPE
Pros:
- Beer, wine, cheese, Apero, festivals
- Afternoon siesta
- Travel quickly and cheaply to many countries around

Cons:
- The most expensive with the value of the euro
- Most countries smoke a lot

NORTH AMERICA
Pros:
- The American dream, capitalism and business mindset
- Big wild animals and national parks
- Clean fresh air

Cons:
- Long bus route to travel from big cities
- Expensive cell phone and internet carrier
- Cold blood as we say, meaning more egocentric

SOUTH AMERICA
Pros:
- The Latino vibe of family spirit and warm blood dancing
- World natural wonders
- Eating good meat
- Fresh organic fruits and vegetables

Cons:
- Expensive to move from countries to countries
- Sense of stress walking at night in the streets because of its robbery stories

ASIA
Pros:
- Introduction to Buddhism and meditation practices
- Cheap and light food
- Cheap flights around the nearby countries
- Paradise beaches & islands

Cons:
- Streets are insoluble
- Pollution

AUSTRALASIA
Pros:
- Most stunning diving coral reef in the world
- Beach lifestyle of bikini and surf

Cons:
- You most likely won't visit other countries
- Expensive

AFRICA
Pros:
- Safari and extreme wildlife

Cons:
- More dangerous and insoluble

Top ten most popular cities to go on exchange:
1. Montreal
2. Barcelona
3. Milan
4. Paris
5. Guadalajara
6. Hong Kong
7. Lisbon
8. Budapest
9. Berlin
10. Tokyo

Top ten world best business and management universities in 2018:
1. Harvard University // Boston; USA
2. INSEAD // Fontainebleau; France
3. London Business School // London; England
4. Massachusetts Institute of Technology (MIT) // Boston, USA
5. University of Pennsylvania // Philadelphia; USA
6. Stanford University // Stanford near San Francisco; USA
7. University of Cambridge // Cambridge; England
8. University of Oxford // Oxford; England
9. London School of Economics and Political Science (LSE) // London; England
10. Bocconi University // Milan; Italy

My Story on That Topic...

To be honest, I'm not proud of that one, but I ended up deciding where I wanted to go based on what other people though was the coolest destination to go. One day, I heard a conversation of three girls at the cafeteria talking about where they would go if they had the chance to go abroad for a semester. One of them screamed Italy and they all went hysterical about how Italy is paradise. The funny part is that all of them had some kind of lame reason why they wouldn't leave on a semester abroad, the common comfort zone white lies dilemma. That moment shocked me and I've decided from that point that I would take action on that dream they were not taking action on.

I knew nothing about Italy or even Europe back then. I was jumping with closed eyes with no preparation, which led me to some funny peripeties that I'll discuss later and I'm sure you'll relate to.

Case Study *(Choosing a Destination)*

PERSONA:	Marcela F. :: 24 years old :: Italian Exchange city: Sydney, Australia
PROBLEM:	Marcela has always dreamed to travel the whole world. For her first big trip, her Erasmus, she decided to put herself as much as possible outside of her comfort zone but with so many options, she didn't know how to choose.
SITUATION:	She decided to do her exchange in another continent with a complete opposite culture. So she shortlisted either South East Asia or South America. She loves the Latino warm blood dancy and the family spirit of South America but also love the Asian food, its wild animals and unique islands.
ACTION PLAN CONT:	To make her choice she decided to list down her passions and choose two country options per continent. South American countries: Colombia Brazil Asian countries: Thailand Japan Hobbies: Dancing, Volleybal, Photography, People, Psychology, Spirituality, Foreign Language, Reading, Hiking, Volunteering

RESULTS:	She ended up deciding that her top 3 choices will be: 1 - Medellin, Colombia 2 - Rio de Janeiro, Brazil 3 - Tokyo, Japan And she got accepted on her first choice to Medellin Colombia EAFIT University.
WISDOM:	Sitting down and doing personality tests and introspection will always provide you more relevant life decisions. In this example, Marcela made sure to match her personality, interest and vision with her exchange destination and it paid off massively on her growth.

Here are three YouTube videos to watch that sell exchange destination:

1. Day in the Life of a Singapore Exchange Student— NUS Dorm/Campus Tour

2. Study Abroad in India - "DARSHAN: India Through American Eyes" (Trailer)

3. 50 Best Places to Study Abroad in the World

7 - THE REQUEST & THE ACCEPTANCE
The stress of doing everything well

This part is worse than applying to any job, a university degree, or any kind of program. Why? Simply because every country is different, tiny different requirements and on top of that your host university might ask for extra little documents. The best way to go over all this is to make your own list and print everything. Then ask your counselor and past exchange student contact if they think you forgot anything. Fill out everything, then ask a friend or family member to help you go over everything a second time to double-check.

Once this is done to the best you could and you deliver your application, you feel relieved. The only thing to do now is to 'pray' you have your first-choice destination.

It's official, you made it! Scream the announcement to your parents and best friends while hugging them so hard to show them what this adventure really means to you. This little gesture will pay off later on when you'll need mental support. At this point, the best advice I can give you is to make this personal news public on whatever suits you best: social media posts, blog, YouTube, vlog, etc. The goal of doing this is committing yourself fully to the experience and really owning it; talking about it makes it more real. On top of that, it might bring you some friends' advice or give inspiration to your friends to do the same.

Now till your exchange, you're going to dream about all kinds of fantasies & possibilities every night till your departure. You'll be living in a state of joy, which the closest synonym is excitement. You'll try to encounter everyone that knows a little about the destination you'll be going. It's good to be daydreaming and visualizing your exchange, but you can easily get stuck too much on the thought patterns of daydreaming and escaping your current reality.

The best tool to help you with this is meditation and the book, *The Power of Now*, by the world-famous Eckhart Tolle, which is the number one spiritual book in the world.

My Story on That Topic...

I got given my second choice because everyone wanted the University of Bocconi in Milan, the best business school in Italy and 3rd in Europe. I was a bit disappointed, but I trusted the universe for the path it was directing me. And out of nowhere, 1–2 months later, I received an email from the international students' office telling me that I was the 3rd on the list and the 2nd person finally decided to cancel his exchange student semester.

How lucky I was to end up receiving one of the only two spots to go experience one of the best universities in the world.

Watch this Tedx Talk of a Spanish student going to Sofia Bulgaria for exchange:

Who should be an Erasmus student | Julia Fernandez Diaz | TEDxNBU

8 - PERSONAL FINANCE
What they should teach us at school

Back then, I received a scholarship of $4000 to go on a four-month semester abroad, plus easily received a student loan of $5500 with a low-interest rate that I needed to pay back only after my studies. But no worries, to any problem, there's a solution. Let me help you find some financing alternatives for your exchange.

Scholarships:

- For sure, your university is offering some kind of international experience mobility scholarship. Search on their website in the scholarship section or the international students' desk section.
- If you are a good student, aim at getting a scholarship of excellence.
- Propose your international students' desk to document and report your exchange from a business development point of view. Documenting the partner university services, the university, the destination, and interviewing other students. Your report should be full of statistics, data, interviews, and examples that they can show to their manager the worth of their investment.
- https://www.gooverseas.com/blog/ study-abroad-scholarships-grants

Sponsorships:

- With this same kind of business development mindset from the scholarships above, approach local startups in your city that might be interested in market research in the country you are going that could help their expansion. A small business case assignment.
- Set your Google Local guide account and start a vlog or a blog to give visibility to companies in your host destination where you'll receive in exchange gratuities like free nights in a dorm room, one-day trips, travel products, free coffee and meals, etc. It's a small investment for a small business to have you review their service. It boosts their SEO and online social proof.

Loans:

- Depending on your country, banks easily give students loans that you repay over ten years after your degree with low interest because they assume and want that after your degree you'll find a corporate job and get stuck into the system.
- https://www.goabroad.com/travel-resources/study-abroad-loans

Students' Jobs:

- Abroad, you should be able to work up to 20 hours a week on the campus with your student visa. Most universities set up this arrangement.

Online Jobs:

- If you have any special skills, create an Upwork or Fiverr profile and hunt those online gigs offerings.
- The whole work system is becoming remote as we need fewer and fewer offices to control employees to do their work. Search for a job on those new remote job marketplaces.
  - https://remote.com/
  - https://remoteok.io/
  - https://remotive.io/
  - https://weworkremotely.com/
  - https://startup.jobs/
  - https://torre.co/
  - https://www.workingnomads.co/
  - https://www.indeed.com/l-Remote-jobs.html
  - https://www.flexjobs.com/
  - https://remote.co/
  - https://jobspresso.co/remote-work/

Your ideal budget:
- Never spend more than 30% of your budget on rent with monthly utilities (internet, phone, electricity, water, cable). Living is your biggest expense.
- 30% on eating and drinking & nightlife. As a student, control your alcohol and club budget.
- 30% of your social life experiences and travel.
- The last 10% savings in case of problems and for the end of your journey gift

Money is an illusion. You don't need it to:
- **GIVE BACK.** Give back your time, knowledge, smile, kindness, and support instead. Money can never help someone with a negative state of mind. Read *Give and Take* by Adam Grant to learn more about this.
- **MAKE AN IMPACT.** Start by becoming the best person you can be, and inspire people around you before you even think of saving the world. Read *Think and Grow Rich* by Napoleon Hill, and *Awaken the Power Within* by Tony Robbins for more advice on this.
- **TRAVEL THE WORLD.** Traveling Southeast Asia with a disciplined budget would cost you no more than $1000-$1500/month, and you could do this while working online and earning extra cash. Read *The 4-Hour Workweek* by Tim Ferriss to know how it's done.
- **PAY YOUR DEBT.** The entire planet is on debt. You just need to know how to manage your debt. Use it as leverage, and don't try to repay it in full before starting to live. Read *Rich Dad, Poor Dad* by Robert T. Kiyosaki, and *The Richest Man in Babylon* by George S. Clason to learn more about how to manage your debt.
- **INVEST IN YOURSELF.** Doing this is almost free with the help of the internet. With all the personal growth

content on YouTube, Podcasts, and Tedx Talks, your goal is to use *the 5 Second Rule* by Mel Robbins to kick yourself in the butt and take tiny constant actions on your learnings. Keep a daily personal growth journal and read *The One Thing* by Gary Keller as a guide in doing this.

- **GET YOUR DREAM HOME, CAR, BIG TOY, OR OTHER MATERIAL WEALTH.** This is a brainwash dream sold by Hollywood and advertisers. It will give you momentary happiness, a dopamine rush, that will fade over time. Seek happiness of your state of mind instead of happiness of your emotion. Read *The Power of Now* by Eckart Tolle to learn how this can be achieved.

Here are five pieces of advice on personal finance to help you start building the right habits NOW:

1. 'Pay Yourself First' concept. Before paying any of your bills (credit cards, loans, utilities, food, rent, etc.), pay yourself by dropping 10% of your income in a close investment bank account. Your goal is to forget about this money like it doesn't exist and then grow it to reach an amount that you'll be able to invest in something with a 10–20% profit, depending on your skills and resources.

2. Invest in self-development 10% of your goal net worth. People who are worth 1 million dollars invested the equivalent of $100,000 worth of self-development products on the same domain to become experts. Buy books, join courses, attend seminars, and live life-changing experiences on the skills that will lead you to the top.

3. Give back 5% of your income. Giving primes your brand to the highest state but do it wisely. Studies show that givers are either right at the bottom of society or way at the top. Put some barriers when giving your time, money, and knowledge to prevent people from taking advantage

of you. Structure it and build the habits. Sponsor a child, volunteer, educate, etc. Find a cause that you are truly attached to. It will even make you want to commit to devoting more time.

4. Change your mindset from a poor person thinking to a rich person thinking. Don't save on cheap food full of chemicals that would immediately deteriorate your health and lower your energy, which could stop you from fully living in the present moment, and impacting your surroundings. Don't lose 10–15 minutes on finding deals and discounts on saving a few dollars. Spend those extra dollars, clear your mind of thoughts, and put your time on learning and acting on becoming a person with better self-worth.

5. Change your words, change your mind. Sit down with a piece of paper and ask yourself, "How can I afford that?" instead of telling yourself, "I can't afford that". Then list down 20 solutions to your problem. This will push you to be creative and help you determine your skills, network, knowledge, and resources in order to know the first small step of action you should take.

Here are three YouTube videos to manage your money, or find a simple online job:

1. I Will Teach You to Be Rich by Ramit Sethi - How You Become Rich Animated Book Summary

2. 9 EASY Online Jobs that Pay Through PayPal (FAST!)

INSPIRATION ▶

Case Study (Budgeting)

Everyone knows that managing personal finance is an essential habit that needs to be built but almost everyone struggle to commit to it. Mismanagement will always drag you to the same hole. You really become in charge of your life when you start building your finance habits.

PERSONA:	Alejandro R. :: 22 years old :: Brazilian Exchange city: Boston, USA University: Harvard | Law
PROBLEM:	Alejandro has one year to finance his exchange in the United States. He's looking for $12500 for 5 months to cover his rent, travel, and social life.
SITUATION:	Savings: None Work: Student job $8/hour 15 hours a week to pay for his lifestyle Scholarship: $5000 from South America Future Leaders Scholarship

ACTION PLAN:	He made a monthly budget of $2500 that he's distributing this way::
	
	       Flat share room rental = $550 Cellphone = $30
	       Metro pass = $40
	       Travel = $800
	       Social Life = $300
	       Grocery + Restaurants = $500
	       Security extra = $280

ACTION PLAN CONT:	He decided to open an investment account to transfer his savings to collect the $7500 missing. 1. Pay himself first 20% of his monthly student job salary to his investment account. $10x15hx-4weeksx20%x12months = $1440 2. He decided to do a garage sale of all his childhood and teenage toys and other stuff sitting in the basement = $500 3. He launched a crowdfunding campaign on Facebook and Kickstarter promising the whole family of aunts and uncles and university friends to reach his dream while sharing entertaining Instagram Stories daily of his exchange journey. = $2000 4. Asked a personal line of credit at his bank backed by the signature of his parents that he will repay in 5 years = $4000 5. Promise his parents that he will start working online 6 hours a week during his exchange. $10x6hx4weeksx4months = $960
RESULTS:	With his plan he is able to gather $8900 Plus his scholarship of $5000 He has 13,$900 to fully live the experience of his life, an investment on himself that will pay in the long run.
WISDOM:	For the first time in life you'll have a big amount of money to manage. Use this opportunity as your simulation to manage your personal finances for the rest of your life. Plan, Budget, Analyze, Pay Yourself First, Give Back, Have an Emergency Bank Account. Don't worry if you ever you missed your budget, you are human, you will learn from it. Plans exist to set intention and give you awareness, it helps you to reflect and improve.

9 - EXCHANGE STUDENT EXPERIENCE GONE BAD
It might be the worst experience of your life

While YouTube is currently invaded by exchange students' stories having the best time of their lives, I stumbled on a catchy video title and then read a few comments that got me thinking. Yes, this experience could be the worst of your life if you don't set your state of mind right, you don't break your comfort zone daily, and you don't have a strong community or organization fulfilling your social life.

It is your responsibility to adapt to your environment depending on your MBTI personality. You're responsible for setting your state of mind every morning with affirmation, journaling and doing sports or anything that gets you moving toward a positive momentum. It is your responsibility to push your comfort zone daily to go say hi and smile at people even if for you the language is a huge barrier. I know that it is easier to say than to be done, but you need to make it part of who you are if you want to mentally survive this experience.

Exchange Student's Story...

One year after doing my exchange, I was advising quite a few people that were about to leave. Sadly, I had been in touch with two guys that seemed to be best friends and were going to the same destination on exchange. To my utmost surprise, they decided to quit their semester abroad to come back home only after 1–2 weeks over there. Spending so much time, energy and money (most likely parents' money here) to finally jump and then not being able to fully push through and end the experience.

That type of behavior builds you on the wrong patterns for life. You telling yourself that it's ok to quit, it doesn't matter what others have done to help you, it's ok to start something and not finish it. I think this type of decisions will haunt you for the rest of your life. It's even worse than not going in the first place. If you end up not being happy with your destination or university you have chosen and your whole situation is a mess, you have no choice to suck it up and at least the learning lessons will be bigger. Time will solve everything and this situation will build you stronger than the norm; it will force you to see the little hidden positive things that require a positive state of mind. Home is not a destination; it's a vibration frequency you emit to attract the right kind of people.

Exchange Student's Story...

This story above is not an isolated case; it happens to many exchange students every semester. I had one case at InterStude were the guy was about to be one of our trip leaders, but I canceled on him last minute before the trip because I had a bad feeling about him. He ended up leaving Montreal one week after with a long Facebook post of excuses trying to convince himself and the world that he was making the right decision to quit and go home to reunite with his girlfriend again.

Exchange Student's Story...

At the time of my exchange in Milan, there was this legendary story going around of an American exchange student on exchange in Barcelona. While apartment hunting, he ended up trusting what seemed to be an apartment tenant. He decided to take this apartment, dropped all his luggage to go do his first grocery shopping, and came back with a massive surprise: the whole apartment was empty. Everything got stolen: his money, passport, luggage, clothes, etc.

He was so desperate that he called his dad that took the big decision to jump on a plane to help his son start from zero. Together, they found a new apartment, bought new clothes, and redid paperwork to freshly start school. I mean what a super hero dad, right?

The moral of this story is that in your darkest moments, you'll connect stronger with the person that you love.

KEYNOTES SUMMARY OF THE CHAPTER:

- Dreaming and chasing a dream is the most fulfilling thing because it leads you to growth

- Everything you wish for is possible. Learn how to manifest your dreams

- By nature, we humans are always looking for comfort, but the best memories will arrive outside of your comfort zone

- Deep research and preparation is the key to maximizing every project in life, and everything is a project

- Each and every one has an ideal destination; find yours

- The best way to speed up your growth and live fully the right experience is to learn to know you're better than anyone else

- Celebrate fully your acceptance to go on exchange

- Personal finance, the taboo skill you'll need to master by yourself before going anywhere in life

- Yes, it's possible to turn this experience into the worst experience of your life, so be in control, be cautious, and don't sabotage yourself

NEXT CHAPTER...

The next chapter talks about planning the experience of your life and coping with the strong emotions of departure. Are you excited? You should, as planning a trip makes people even happier than doing the actual trip because excitement gives you hope, joy, and energy.

EXPERT
INTERVIEW :: **Colin Riendeau**

https://www.linkedin.com/in/colinriendeau/

Short film producer from New York, studied Specialization Communication at Concordia University in Montreal.

American born with a Quebecois father. Came to Montreal learning French from scratch.

PERSONAL & BUSINESS BIO

Founder of No Water Studios http://www.nowaterstudios.com/

In business since 2013, social media video campaign and short film production. The biggest project so far has been the creation of the short film 'The Fish' combining ten actors, ten film locations, and a crew of almost 100 people.

Here's the movie trailer https://vimeo.com/191337668

THE ERASMUS MARKET

Why is it important to learn about culture for someone that has never traveled? If you have never traveled, you've never experienced the world in a different way. You've never experienced the difference in how other people think. For business, it is crucial to getting creative ideas from what others are doing. An example is the automobile industry where my European friend is stating that the USA is ten years behind on manufacturing technology mainly because most Americans don't travel.

What are the top skills that this global citizen mindset gives you? One of the top things is being comfortable being uncomfortable. Being open to pushing yourself out of your comfort zone. Other skills are language and taking risks, being open to failing.

Why do exchange students party so much? You only have one experience, you only have one life. With that kind of short experience, you want to get out the most of it. Human beings are social in nature. One of the ways for people to break the barrier of society while constructing humans bound in a foreign setting is having fun through entertainment. I relearnt the majority of my French through partying. Also, there's a lot of stress that comes with that new foreign setting, and one of the ways to release it is through alcohol.

What are your best tips to live the international roommates' lifestyle? You need to be okay with a messy kitchen. More diversified are your roommates coming from different parts of the world, which you'll learn about yourself. At the end of the day, it makes you want to change, being more flexible.

THE ENTREPRENEURSHIP MINDSET

What are the best advices you've got from high individuals? When I was 18 years old working in Los Angeles, while exhausted from long working hours, the producer asked me how I felt. I responded, "Actually, I feel pretty shitty". The producer responded, "Remember how that feels because one day you'll be in a position to call the shots and inspire the younger generation and you'll need to put yourself in their shoes".

Colin ends up giving his own advice: "The decision-makers are just normal human beings, so don't be starstruck when approaching them. If you could treat them like you don't need anything from them and truly connect on other subjects than your professional goals, you'll go a long way".

When you think of success, who is the first person that comes to mind? A guy from high school class that has always been driven by the success sold by society. After going to university, he realized the trap and shifted his whole perspective 180 degrees around. Success is doing what you are passionate about and being the best version of the person you can be for yourself. There's nothing wrong with being a successful father without focusing on your professional life. Everyone should have their own definition of success.

What are your next big goals to move forward toward your success? Continue moving forward on improving and keeping strong routines, accepting setbacks, and building a stronger mindset to face failures. I have three big projects currently, working on two feature films and one short film while managing smaller projects to keep some cash flow.

What are the books you refer the most? *Deep Survival* by Laurence Gonzales

My number one book, because it focuses on the mental process that people have in a survival situation. Applicable in your travel life, putting yourself outside of your comfort zone, and how to deal with stress in the work environment.

CONCLUSION

Happiness is...my favorite pastry and morning espresso.

Life is...beautiful and difficult.

A real entrepreneur is...like climbing a mountain full of obstacles, setbacks, and once you get to the top, you realize it was an amazing journey.

A good traveler is...someone who is open to new experiences, perceptive, intuitive, and not an obsequious jackass.

An international student is...a wild party monster who has an interesting perspective or view of the world that makes some difference to move it forward.

The worst thing you can do for the world is...avoid single-use plastic items.

CHAPTER 2

The Departure

THE INNOCENCE BEFORE

1 - 2 TYPES OF PEOPLE: LOCAL AND GLOBAL CITIZEN

The Global Citizens revolution has started

There are two types of university students: the local and the global citizen. The local is stuck into a college degree their parents sent them to, overly watch sports, TV, Netflix, and is a consumer of the system - getting a car, house, overspending on clothes, etc. The global citizen escapes the status quo and decides to spend money on experiences, invests in himself, is driven to make an impact during his lifetime and believes that no matter our skin color, accent, and background, we are all part of the same nation and that we are one.

Congratulations! By jumping into this new life-changing experience, you have become a Global Citizen, if you were not already one. Global Citizens are the brightest aspiration we have to improve the earth and our civilization. As a Global Citizen, you start by having a sense of multiple nationalities, then you identify yourself as to having global citizenship, you start to get involved in social enterprises and nonprofits and then you create your own impact project.

2 - THE NON-ACCEPTANCE OF YOUR LOVED ONES
No one thinks you'll make the jump

At this point, you've already started to live on another planet than your loved ones. You try to share your excitement with them and expect them to be excited for you too. Very few humble people will step back and try to put themselves in your shoes. It is at this point that the mental battle starts from lacking true moral support.

Obviously, this will differ from your Myers–Briggs Type Indicator (MBTI) personality and how close you and your parents are as they raised you. I highly recommend for you to discover and identify your MBTI personality as well as the one of your parents and siblings for you to become more aware of their strengths and weaknesses. Also, knowing their love languages goes a long way in showing your love, empathy, and appreciation, especially in times of conflict or misunderstanding. You get what you give. We are one and the same. When you smile at them, you smile to yourself. When you give love to them, you give yourself love.

My Story on That Topic...

That moment in time is engraved on my head, I remember precisely being so excited to announce that I've been accepted on an exchange program and I was going abroad. As I arrived home from university, I entered my mom's house, saw her in the kitchen, jumped towards the other side of the counter where she was cooking, and said, "You know what? I'm going on exchange in Europe!" She responded, "You? Going abroad? Is it a joke?" I can still remember that facial expression on her; she thought I would never be able to jump.

As more time passed, you would like to spend more quality time not just with your family, but also friends with thoughts that you won't be seeing them for a while. You just want to stop time, but on their end, they are stuck into their daily grind of activities and their own worries. Sadly, this is the moment you realize that things will never be the same and you'll somehow lose your home and friends as you knew it.

"YOU WILL NEVER BE AT HOME AGAIN. BECAUSE PART OF YOUR HEART WILL ALWAYS BE ELSEWHERE. THAT IS THE PRICE YOU PAY FOR THE RICHNESS OF LOVING AND KNOWING PEOPLE IN MORE THAN ONE PLACE."

~ MIRIAM ADENEY

3 - ZERO STRESS ONE MONTH BEFORE
You close your eyes on what is coming

There are two types of people: the one who will plan and the one who won't plan and just go with the flow. I was part of the latter, but today I wished I could have planned at least a little bit. The non-planners avoid the stress of a big day by leaving everything last minute. But there's a better way to manage that stress. The goal is to take tiny actions daily.

Use the Kaizen principle of setting yourself the tiniest daily goals to achieve, and with repetition over time, you'll gain the habit of it. More precisely, it takes 66 days to build a habit into a lifestyle. What we are trying to create here is a habit of daily planning for the days ahead. Whenever doubts creep in on starting your daily planning, just use *the 5 second rule* to trick your mind that is hesitating. The moment you sense you are hesitating, start counting backward 5, 4, 3, 2, 1. Like mentioned before, it freezes the rational thinking of your prefrontal cortex, this is when you take deliberate action.

Watch this amazing Tedx Talk on how we are all the same leaving things to the last minute:

Inside the mind of a master procrastinator | Tim Urban

CHECKLIST ON THE MINIMUM YOU SHOULD DO ONE MONTH BEFORE LEAVING:

- ☐ Photocopy your passport and immigration letters.

- ☐ Search the best neighborhood to live and create a wish list of a potential apartment to visit in your first days.

- ☐ Find your bed to sleep for your first five nights (hostel, Airbnb, a friend of friend's couch).

- ☐ Screenshot the Google map itinerary from the airport to your 1st-night accommodation.

- ☐ Know when is the most important welcome event to meet your fellow exchange students.

- ☐ Find the best company to buy a sim card and prepaid data package to help you with Google maps or Uber in case you get lost.

- ☐ Create a monthly expenses budget depending on your finance.

- ☐ Create a first draft calendar plan of your four months' exchange doing tours, events, and cultural experiences.

- ☐ Go take a coffee with one of the students in your city that went to the same destination on exchange.

4 - TWO DAYS BEFORE LEAVING
The Panic

You just had your goodbye party and the stress starts to rush in. *What if this happens, what if that happens, what if I forget something?* So much tiny fears just keep on rushing in. People ask you if you are excited, but your soul is empty from the mix of dozens of emotions. You need to think, relax, and master the basics.

Okay, what do I need to do? First, tell yourself that you are not alone; millions of people have passed by this before you and they've figured it out. Meditate, and after doing so, start repassing over your planning.

5 - PACK YOUR BAGS LIKE A MINIMALIST TRAVEL MASTER.
Less is More. The Less You Bring, the Less You Have to Lose and the Less You Have to Worry About.

TIPS FOR YOUR 23KG:

- ☐ Lay everything you want to bring on your bed so that you can see the whole picture.

- ☐ Try to eliminate about a third, which is very conservative because either way, you'll wear 80% of the time 20% of your clothes following Pareto's Law.

- ☐ Organize all clothing per type and put the items in vacuum storage or compression bags so you save space.

- ☐ Start filling your suitcase with the bigger bags first like the plastic bag of jeans and the plastic bag of sweatshirts.

- [ ] Leave some space in the middle of the suitcase to maximize protection for the non-clothing items like books, cameras, toiletries, chargers, etc.

- [ ] Don't forget to pack the lifesavers: a transformer charger, a small umbrella or a poncho, a thin raincoat, a selfie stick, Bluetooth speaker, a phone battery pack, earplugs, laundry bag, swimming hat for public pools, etc.

- [ ] Adjust what you need depending on the weather of the country you are going to live for four months minimum, do your research. Also, it might be cheaper to buy or rent the extra stuff in that country.

TIPS FOR YOUR 10KG:

- [ ] All your main electronics, like your laptop in a case or your professional camera.

- [ ] Headphones with a jack to watch the plane movies, phone chargers and a phone battery pack to make sure you always have batteries on your phone.

- [ ] All your immigration and citizenship documents.

- [ ] Your self-development journal to introspect during the flight.

- [ ] A toothbrush and travel toothpaste, a 100ml deodorant, moisturizing cream, and cleaning wipes to clean a bit yourself during the layover.

- [ ] Your best self-development book (hopefully the *Exchange Your Life* book) or a travel book.

- [ ] Snacks like walnuts, apples, protein bars, and gum when your ears pop, and water bottle to save money.

☐ A sleeping mask, earplugs, and if you like an inflatable pillow.

I think it's really worth the investment if you can afford to get those trendy travel expert famous Nomatic Travel Backpacks for $269 or from one of their travel bag competitors. Search for a comparison website.

☐ Visualize your Departure and Arriving using Google map street view and recording the steps you need to take in case you won't have internet.

☐ Manage your fears.

Everyone knows that they need to face their fears to become their best version. Easy to say when you can consciously identify them like the fear of heights, fear of tarantula, fear of flying, etc. But the truth is that your biggest fears blocking you are hidden in your subconscious. For example, the fear of abandonment from your romantic relationship, a fear that is most likely coming from an abandoned situation you experienced with your parents or friends when you were less than seven years old. Another common example is the fear of vulnerability from not looking like a failure, being afraid of what others think of you, which might be coming from your cultural conditioning.

To find those subconscious hidden fears, you have no choice but to go deep within. Analyze your beliefs, your conditioning, the patterns of negative emotions you always go back to. Know yourself deeply with the *Become Your Best Version* workbook, find your trapped emotions, and do a few of the 22 life experiences, listed in the spirituality sub- section, that will make you meet your soul.

It's also extremely useful to plan on how to overcome your fears. List down the top fears you have now that are stopping you from growing to your best self. Start the sentence with, "What if I...lose my parents, quit my job, leave my relationship, miss my public speaking gig, jump from a plane, do ayahuasca, travel the world for one year, quit college, start a business, don't pay my debt, etc."

Go in-depth watching this video, "Why you should define your fears instead of your goals | Tim Ferriss TedTalk"

Here's the technique in details:

DEFINE. What if I...(list your fear happening)

Really ask yourself why you are feeling that way to arrive at the bottom core.

Write ten worst things that would happen.

PREVENT. How can you prevent these episodes? Or decrease the likelihood of them happening?

REPAIR. Repair. What could I do to repair the damage if my fear happens? Is there anyone else in the history of time who has figured this out? What would be the benefits of an attempt or partial success? What are the possible good outcomes if you take action?

COST OF INACTION. If I avoid these actions, what would my life look like? (emotionally, physically, financially, etc. - in six months, In one year, In three years)

"THE FEARS WE DON'T FACE BECOME OUR LIMITS."

~ ROBIN SHARMA

We have six basic fears that combine them all. You can go in-depth in the masterpiece book, *Think and Grow Rich* by Napoleon Hill which is commonly known to be the source of 90% of all modern self-development books today and also stated as the number one book that influenced the lives of 80% of guests of Tim Ferriss Podcast.

Named in the order of their most common appearance, the first three are at the bottom of one's worries:

Fear of poverty (symptoms: indifference, indecision, doubt, worry, over-caution, procrastination, and refusal to accept responsibility when it can be avoided)

Fear of criticism (symptoms: self-consciousness through nervousness and timidity of conversation, lack of poise, personality, inferiority complex, extravagance, lack of initiative, and lack of ambition)

Fear of ill health (symptoms: negative autosuggestion, hypochondria, proper physical exercise, susceptibility, self-coddling, and intemperance)

Fear of loss of the love of someone (symptoms: jealousy, fault finding, and gambling)

Fear of old age (symptoms: the tendency to slow down and develop an inferiority complex, the habit of speaking apologetically of one's self as "being old", the habit of killing off initiative, imagination, and self-reliance)

Fear of death (symptoms: thinking about dying instead of making the most of life, generally, to lack of purpose, or lack of suitable occupation)

Here are some self-analysis test questions that can help you identify consciously hidden fears:

1. Do you deliberately avoid the association of anyone, and if so, why?

2. Are you envious of those who excel before you?
3. Who has the most inspiring influence upon you? What is the cause?
4. Do you form your own opinions or permit yourself to be influenced by other people?
5. Do you have a definite major purpose, and if so, what is it and what plan do you have for achieving it?
6. Do you rely on liquor, narcotics, or cigarettes to "quiet your nerves?"

In Traditional Chinese Medicine, five main emotions get blocked in five yin-organs. Joy in the heart, grief or anxiety in the lungs, pensiveness in the spleen, anger in the liver, and fear or fright in the kidneys. Linked emotions to fears are weak willpower, insecurity, aloofness (detached, antisocial, introverted), and isolation (minimal contact with others). Physical symptoms are lower back pain, dry mouth, premature grey hair, premature ejaculation, nocturnal emission, etc. All your deepest fears unmanaged as a kid literally get stuck into your kidneys, and all that energy blockage rips off tissues in the long run leading to potential deep disease or cancer as you grow old.

The most common way to release that qi (vital energy) is acupuncture and herbs like Rehmannia, Lycii and Schisandra. Also, eating certain foods help the kidney, like kidney beans, black sesame seeds, walnuts, protein, asparagus, eggs, sweet potato, seaweed string beans, celery, parsley, grapes, plums, berries, and sea salt.

Emotions energy blockage is at the core of every disease. Don't wait 'til you're 40 or 50. Heal yourself now by starting your spiritual journey, trying holistic alternative medicine and meditating daily. Watch the new Netflix documentary, 'Heal', to start your journey.

My Story of the Topic:

Why am I telling you about all this? After 5-6 years stuck in my business with no growth while facing problems after problems trying to find a solution on improving the business domain per domain, I ran out of ideas on how to get myself out of the hole. At that place, after another big failure, I realized I was the problem and I was internally messed up. Through my readings, I stumbled on things like, "To real move your business from a small business (10-30 members) to a real organization (50+ members), you need to become a leader, a leader that inspires others by his extraordinary example". Or things like, "Your business problems are four times heavier emotionally when you don't fix your personal problems". Or things like, "A business' worth will never outgrow the self-worth of the some of his owners".

Through those awakening perspectives, I started to dive deep on the psychological path of Who Am I? What is my personality traits? What am I really good at? What do I truly want? Deep tests, introspections, life planning that led me to so many incredible discoveries about myself, my beliefs, my thoughts, my patterns, my relationship with myself and others, and so much more.

All that work led me to building the *Become Your Best Version* workshop and I've met so many incredible guests attending and sharing their stories. Stories that led me toward my spiritual path exploring for the first time the 5th dimension (the spirit realm), my energetic body, my soul, my emotions trapped, my birth process, my connections to time, my past lives and understanding God the divine light. Without that spiritual path, I would still be trapped in the same crazy eight loop craving business success for admiration of others, fame, money, recognition as I was for most of my adult life.

5 - THE DEPARTURE
Emotional loneliness

"Flying to the unknown", this feeling will become a drug in the future, trust me. Being all by yourself in an airport, watching people being stressed for missing their flights or by packing too much, watching thousands of lives unfold with the same patterns while you are there thinking about your past life that you'll never experience again. You stop time to remember the good days, to be grateful for your journey, to mentally smile at what your loved ones did or said in the last months. This moment when you take the plane alone to change your life is like passing to the next level, your next level to become more—more mature, more conscious, more peaceful. The best analogy is that you have just finished a level in a video game and you are finally stepping up to a higher, harder level. Record your thoughts because there will be so many, so deep, so self-revealing. And 1–2 years would need to pass for you to truly understand all your thoughts at this time.

☐ Buy a new book or magazine at the airport book store.

At this point, your brain is so conscious like the universe is speaking to you. Go to the airport book store and scan with your eyes wide open the self-development books, travel books, travel magazines, and entrepreneur magazines. Trust that you'll have something special that will pop in your face like it's telling you "I'm the one!" Buy it. I had my best reads and life-changing swift perspectives finding magical reads like that.

Slowly by acting this way and being fully mindful of your surroundings, you'll start seeing patterns of the Synchronicity Concepts, originally coined by Carl Jung, to describe meaningful coincidences—the "acausal connecting principle" that links mind and matter, superseding cause and effect.

☐ Take some plane selfie-and thoughts vlogging.

Freeze this moment in time by taking a selfie with the plane behind on departure or arrival. This is going to be the photo where you'll look at someday and tell yourself, "This is the day that I exchanged my life."

☐ Maximize this crucial period in time to start your exchange journal.

New York Time Best Selling author Tim Ferriss, in his most recent book, *Tools of Titans*, which features his past 200 podcast interviews of billionaires, icons, and world-class performers, realized that all those successful people had three habits in common: meditation, journaling, and having a life coach or mentor.

Personally building a strong daily habit of journaling is by far the habit I'm most proud of and that I can't recommend enough. You'll pass 3–4 journals per year, and over the years, there will come that day when you'll explore them back again. You'll realize how deeply you have grown, you'll remember deep thoughts and memories that will bring you back to your true essence and make you cry of gratitude and joy for the journey of bumpy rides you had that led you to who you are today.

Here's all the content you can explore in your journal:
- **Stream of consciousness writing also called 750 words morning pages.** Let your thoughts flow on the paper without letting the pen stop touching the journal. You can't stop five seconds to think of what you'll write; just write whatever words that come. Be the instrument of the universe.
- **Evening journaling.** Brain-dump all ideas and emotions before going to sleep. List down three amazing things that happened today. Write what you are excited about tomorrow; it will help you get up on fire.
- **Monthly Feedback.** Use the end of the journal for that. At the end of each month, recap your accomplishment per cycle of life dimensions (Job, Business, Personal, Physical, Spiritual, Finance, Relationships). Things that you did, that happened, that you are proud of, your wins. And also list 2–3 goals for each dimension for the next month.
- **Gratitude statements.** Every morning, write down three things you are most grateful for. Go into the most little tiny things, God is in the details.
- **Affirmations.** List down daily three affirmations starting with, "I AM...loved, grateful, confident, sexy, playful, a giver, etc."
- **Creative writing.** Draft an article idea that it's your head or poem or why not the script of your next public speaking speech.

- **Travel Exploration memories.** You don't need to be rich to travel; sometimes a small escape outside the town will give you that same feeling. Go on and write down about those feelings you lived while exploring something new. The positive stories will bring you joy for days.
- **Notes of podcasts and books.** Write down your golden nuggets takeaway from the book you are reading now. List your core concepts you need to work on. Quotes, ideas, key phrases you would like to remember coming out of your daily learning habit.
- **Planning.** I like to use the end of the journal for that. Plan your week, your month and most importantly, your year. I highly suggest that you transcribe those plans into a Google doc that you print to always remind and push yourself.
- **Daily Goals.** List down three goals that if you accomplish today will make you grow to the next level.
- **Introspection exercise.** Again, I like to use the end of the journal for that. This can be any introspection exercise you stumble on in your research or book reading. You can get my top 20+ introspection in the *Become Your Best Version* workbook.
- **Dream reading.** Set your journal open with a pen ready on a table next to your bed. The moment your mind and senses open, pull out all the strength you have to write everything you can remember. Colors, symbols, animals, person, location, settings, smell. Everything is important. It is not so much in the story but the things that symbolize something for your real life. Connect with the universe to guide you towards the right path.
- **Keeping a copy of your 3-year vision.** Print a copy of the 3-year vision you did in the *Become Your Best Version* workbook and keep it in your journal that you read daily. Also,

go ahead writing more details of that vision during your daily journaling; it will enhance the law of attraction.

- **Strategy writing.** This idea is coming from Jim Rohn. On the day that you want to quit, that you are exhausted and you just want to shift your life, write down first, what is not working. Second, the barriers that are coming up. Third, ten other ideas you can do to improve per barriers. Finally, end the exercise with affirming "I will not quit" and other top motivation affirmations, then list down the top habit, you can implement to change your life.

- **Days without writing.** There are going to be days that you skip on writing. It's okay, don't be too hard on yourself, we are all humans, and you can still go back on track. That moment you get back on journaling, list down all the dates you've missed and list one thing that you can remember from each day. A feeling, an event, a positive thing, etc. These will help you get back on track.

- **Releasing emotions letters.** Write a fully open letter to someone you still have some misunderstanding or mis-communication with. Write down all your truth that you feel right now. Let go of the negative emotions, the things they have done to you, the things that you wish they would understand, the things that you regret saying or doing. Let everything out. Obviously, you won't send that emotional letter to that person, but it will help you be more at peace with the person and situation.

"WHEN WRITING THE STORY OF YOUR LIFE, DON'T LET ANYONE ELSE HOLD THE PEN."

~ JACK KEROUAC

KEYNOTES SUMMARY OF THE CHAPTER:

- You are a Global citizen now, embrace it.

- Don't expect anything from anyone, don't let others' thoughts affect your vibration.

- Do the minimum one month before, don't wait for the last week before departure.

- The departure, manage your stress, your joy and jump.

- You are leaving, be at peace and enjoy the ride, the universe is on your side.

NEXT CHAPTER...

Landing on a new planet being disoriented, scared and tired wanting a comfy bed? Are you ready? It's going to be hard, but you'll become stronger. No worries, I have the best tips to stay on top of the emotional roller coaster.

EXPERT
INTERVIEW :: Jan Skrjanec

https://www.linkedin.com/in/jan-skrjanec-6a980760/
Entrepreneur from Slovenia, studied Entrepreneurship at
Gea College
Went on exchange to Prague, Czech Republic

PERSONAL & BUSINESS BIO

How did you get started? My experience as a tour leader for a
tour operator in Slovenia brought me to the event industry. During
my exchange in Prague, I started promoting parties that eventually
led to an opportunity to create a boat party. Slowly, I realized that
the Erasmus market was untapped and started promoting the boat
party to international exchange students.

Founder of Erasmus Nation
https://erasmusnation.com/event/spring-break-island/
Location in three cities: Prague, Budapest, Krakow
Currently doing 2500 passengers on 5 events a year

The initial idea was to do a summit with education sightseeing and
conference ending up the day with parties. Over time, we realized
the educational part was not interesting for the Erasmus market
and now it's more of a big weekend trip with Erasmus coming from
all over Europe. The trip has a lot of animation and sightseeing.

Founder of Spring Break Island https://www.springbreakisland.de/
Location: Novalja, Croatia
Currently doing 5000 passengers on one event a year

I merged as partners with the old tour operator I worked for before college which had this nice product but was lacking the community and I brought the market in.

THE ERASMUS MARKET

Why do you think exchange students party so much? You get in a group or community of the same thinking. For most of them, it's the first time they don't have parental control. They go out and they just relax, they just party. And most of the time, they can afford more because drinking in Europe is cheaper.

As examples, the Israelis take a gap year off after college, to relax and go all in before joining the army while Americans travel to a spring break destination where they go bananas and go back home after and be good students again.

Did you discover any passions or hobbies during your exchange? I started my first business on my own. Entrepreneurship has always been there, but I took action at that time. I always had in mind the famous "Pursue your dreams" and when you are 22–23 years there's not much at stake.

What is your best memory in exchange? Hanging out with this very nice Belgian girl that I have fallen in love with.

How was your post-Erasmus depression? I didn't really have it because of my past summer job of working in the Greece islands living in paradise and then going home for fall. I got used to that feeling.

What was your cultural shock when you arrived in Prague? Not so much during my Erasmus because I lived in a small bubble only with the Erasmus students. But after when coming back to create my business, it was a challenge to work with the Czech people.

Why do people need to go on Erasmus? The only thing I regret from my Erasmus was that I didn't do it before. I went at 23, but I think 21 years old is the right time.

What are your best tips for exchange students? Save money before to not stress with that, to relax and enjoy.

Choose the right destination. Needs to be a city that gives you a lot of opportunities to travel.

Build a strong community of Erasmus students.

Erasmus is all about instant decisions; don't think, take action.

How are friendships from Erasmus? You assume you'll meet after Erasmus, visit them, or even do a big post-Erasmus reunion. But most friendships are instant friendships that fade away after Erasmus.

How you heard about the Erasmus experience and why did you choose Prague? Heard about it from word to mouth and that I could receive a scholarship. Barcelona, Amsterdam and Prague, my three choices, were destinations I had been before and I had friends that could show me around.

THE ENTREPRENEURSHIP MINDSET

What has been your most challenging situation in business so far? For me, it's how to grow. Creating a business with over 50-100 employees and big investors, and making an exit.

What is the best advice you ever got? Don't waste your time over-thinking. Do what you think is right, and no matter what, 90% of the time you'll be wrong. If you look back, you would do it differently. The most important is the efficiency, the shortest possible time you can make decisions. That's why reunions are useless.

Who inspires you? Every entrepreneur in my surrendering that can influence me.

What are your best skills? I can connect the dots to shape a product with the best partners and market.

Do you have a habit you are proud of? I respect my words all the time no matter what.

If you had 10 million dollar today, what would you do? Create a very big festival.

What is your best advice for a 20-something entrepreneur? Go work for an entrepreneur, let him do all the mistakes, and learn from them. The best moment to launch a business is around 30-35 when you are really mature.

What book would you like to suggest? Every book is a great book if you can take the principle and test them into your business.

I like, *The Business of Expertise: How Entrepreneurial Experts Convert Insight to Impact + Wealth* by David C. Baker - good book on how to find yourself and building a business you are really good at.

Before you die, what would be the three truths to be shared with your loved ones? Be proud and honest, my most important virtue.

Love without control, love with your heart not with your mind.

Travel, traveling is the only thing that gets me into another state of mind.

What is your best advice for the next generation? Don't try to overgrow your age.

CONCLUSION

Happiness is...LIFE.

Life is...people that care.

A good traveler is...a relaxed one.

True entrepreneurs are...those that are able to see profit for everyone involved, not only themselves.

Success is...achieving what you aim for, your vision.

The future is...there and exactly defined. You can't beat the future, you can't affect it because we always try the best in the moment in time with the values and knowledge we have in that moment.

CHAPTER 3 :

The Shock

YOU NEVER DEAL WITH THIS KIND OF INNER DISTURBANCE

1 - THE ARRIVAL, THE FIRST DAY
But in what world have I just landed

This is the time you'll feel out of your comfort zone the most. From the moment you arrive at the airport, everything is different. The people, the interior design, the signs, the restaurants, the shops, etc. Remember this specific moment and how your brain is working. You are experiencing total presence of mind. Just like how Eckhart Tolle explained in his famous book, *The Power of Now*, mindfulness in daily life is like a child walking the streets and looking side to side, up and down, with his eyes right open being amazed by every little detail. This is how we should be constantly living our lives, free of thoughts of the past or future, embracing the moment.

Unfortunately, that feeling doesn't last long; soon, you'll need to get back and figure out, 'How am I going to do this?'

☐ Go get your luggage.

☐ Go to the tourist office to get a physical map and quick insights about the understanding of the main areas.

☐ Buy a prepaid sim card with data right now at the airport if you can.

☐ Go buy your bus/train ticket to go downtown and make sure you understand exactly where to go from there to your place.

☐ Make a friend in the bus/train to break the ice. It doesn't matter who he or she is. Talk to an old person if you want; it's easier. You'll feel so much better and comfortable after breaking that ice.

2 - HOUSING SEARCH
This is hell, the worst part

It has been mentioned before, the best thing to do is to research before departure, create a wish list and prepare some visits, book a place for the first five nights while you get accustomed to the city, and visit apartments. Or even better, if you can afford it, pass by an agency, it's totally worth the cost instead of doing all the research and contacting people. Finding a new place can take 30–40 hours times $20/h (estimation of your time worth), that's $400.

Top 4 websites to find a place for your first 5 days.
- https://fr.airbnb.ca/

- https://www.hostelworld.com/
- https://www.agoda.com
- https://www.couchsurfing.com/

The worst thing you can do here is to have high expectations on the location, apartment space, roommates type, etc. Please don't do that, it'll kill you. Tell yourself, "Let the universe unfold, everything is going just as it was supposed to". No matter what place or who you would end up with, there's definitely going to be some life lessons you'll carry through.

First of all, here are the pros and cons of living in an apartment versus a student residence.

LIVING IN A STUDENT RESIDENCE.
Pros:
- You'll make friends so fast
- You'll never be bored because you can go visit a friend in one minute
- You'll have the best social life ever from the daily events or gatherings
- You won't need to worry about the utilities, cleaning, apartment fixing problems

Cons:
- You'll overpay for accommodation, money you could spend on traveling
- You'll miss the family bonding of living in a flatshare

LIVING IN AN APARTMENT WITH INTERNATIONAL ROOMMATES.

Pros:

- You'll create bond with people for a lifetime; they will feel like family
- Dinner night where a roommate is cooking his country's favorite dish for all the roomies
- Cheaper than living in a student residence
- Have a more comfy room with decoration and details

Cons:

- You could have a more active social life in a student residence

The best option, if you can make it happen, is to take your first month at the student residence to become part of their community and experience this social life and then move to an apartment with roommates to experience the family lifestyle of close human connections.

WHAT TO LOOK FOR IN A GREAT ROOM FLATSHARING:

☐ 20+mbps wifi to support all roommates streaming videos and films.

☐ Real walls in your room with good isolation or sound-proofing. From seeing photos, it is very hard to tell. There are so many people now trying to make money renting rooms and creating extra rooms in apartments with floating walls. No privacy, you hear everything, you can't sleep and have no window.

☐ A cleaning plan structure with the roommates or having a cleaning lady.

☐ A good washing machine not ruining your clothes.

☐ A good kitchen with every appliance needed so that you can cook and save money. Food is your second biggest expense, save money here to travel more.

☐ Enough bathrooms for the amount of roommates (5+ people should have 2+ bathrooms).

☐ A good mattress as you like it and where you can't feel the spring. There's nothing worse than sleeping on a bad mattress; you end up with back pain and become sleepy and moody all the time. Jump on the bed when visiting.

☐ Great roommates fitting your lifestyle, interests, personalities (see the list below).

☐ Great location for your needs (see the list below).

☐ A good owner/tenant that is polite, respects your privacy, and is there for you when needed in less than 48 hours.

- ☐ No more than 20 minutes away from your university. Studies have shown that 20+ minutes of transport to and from your daily workplace can lead to depression.

- ☐ Have a window, obviously.

- ☐ Not mandatory, but surely helps the social life with roommates: having a nice balcony with a view in the apartment.

WHAT TO LOOK FOR IN GREAT ROOMMATES:

- ☐ Other exchange students and at least one local.

- ☐ Matching your best two MBTI personality match (Google search MBTI relationship chart).

- ☐ Having at least one similar passion.

- ☐ Not having one random older, geekier, awkward roommate that breaks all the vibe.

- ☐ Don't have more than four roommates if you are an introvert since it can block you from really feeling comfortable with the apartment.

WHAT TO LOOK FOR IN A GREAT LIVING NEIGHBORHOOD:

- ☐ Maximum 20 minutes away from school on public transportation, as studies have shown that more can lead to depression.

- ☐ Having all the essentials in a walking distance: grocery or convenience store, metro station, coffee shop to take a break or study.

- ☐ Not too noisy, but not too far from the action.

- ☐ Not close to a highway or airport to keep the peaceful vibe.

HERE'S A LIST OF WEBSITES TO SEARCH ROOMS:
For your temporary space on arrival:
https://fr.airbnb.ca/
https://www.hostelworld.com/
https://www.agoda.com

AGENCY SERVICES:
https://www.uniplaces.com/
https://www.spotahome.com/
https://housinganywhere.com/
https://www.spareroom.com

ROOMMATES FINDER:
https://www.easyroommate.com/
https://roomiapp.com

FREE CLASSIFIED ADS WEBSITE LIKE
https://www.kijiji.ca/
https://craigslist.org

MEETING LOCAL PEOPLE ON ARRIVAL:
https://www.meetup.com
https://www.couchsurfing.com/
Facebook rent room groups

My Story on That Topic...

In Milan, I had a challenging room-hunting experience that definitely made up a big part of my cultural shock.

My school put me in contact with a girl from my home university that was already there in Milan one semester for one-year exchange. I contacted her for some advice and she openly welcomed me to stay on her couch a few days while I could find an apartment. Nicest girl ever, she was so excited to welcome me and showed me around. That feeling of showing everything you love and have learned about your second home is incredible.

I had the best arrival welcome days, but my lack of preparation got the most of me. I couldn't find a room to stay because of the high season and all the students managed to arrive in town a few weeks in advance for their apartment-hunting.

After a few days sleeping on Anne's couch with her Italian boyfriend, I really felt I had to leave as soon as possible because I was interfering in their private space and couple's life. I ended up going to the international students' desk begging them to negotiate for me with the main student residence that I can stay there for one month without contract by the time school starts and I find a place to stay. I just couldn't afford the student residence price and didn't want to commit to their contract.

It took me another two weeks to find a place near the school that was not too expensive because I was sharing a big room, probably an old living room. It was an old Italian apartment in a building complex with three Italian guys. They ended up being very cool guys interested in my culture, the world and practicing their English. 'Til this day, they are family to me and I can't wait to see them again in person. Meeting them again in Milan at the best aperitivo in town would be the cherry on the sundae.

Exchange Student's Story...

One year after starting InterStude, I teamed up with the Québécois I met and welcomed in Milan. I showed him around on my last week, his first week of exchange in Milan. We created this Auberge Espagnole flat sharing in Montreal with five rooms, and semester after semester for three years, we hosted three new exchange students from different parts of the world.

It was one of the most profound things I've done in my life. Living as a community, sharing every piece of our personal lives with one other, young souls discovering themselves. So much deep memories. Some roommates become an extension of your family; no matter how far apart you are or how long you don't talk to them nothing would change. You'll reunite for one night where you'll feel fully present in the conversation being so grateful for the time you have passed together, the good and the bad times.

Yes, some roommates' habits will bring the worst headaches in you, but it is with those times that you actually become more aware and realize your own patterns or things you don't want and learn to love people the way they are. Everyone has their equal good and bad side like the whole universe, just like the balance in Yin and Yang philosophy, "the concept of dualism describing how seemingly opposite or contrary forces may actually be complementary, interconnected, and interdependent in the natural world, and how they may give rise to each other as they interrelate to one another"[1].

---

[1] https://en.wikipedia.org/wiki/Yin_and_yang

HERE'S A BUCKET LIST OF THINGS TO DO WITH YOUR INTERNATIONAL ROOMMATES:

- [ ] Brand the apartment with a name and nickname for each roommate.

- [ ] Do a potluck dinner where everyone cooks his respective national dish/es.

- [ ] Cook altogether a massive festive dinner for 20+ friends.

- [ ] Do a movie night all together.

- [ ] Take group dancing classes with a private teacher coming to the apartment.

- [ ] Have each roommate decorate his room door.

- [ ] Do a cremaillere (housewarming) party.

- [ ] Create a Spotify playlist of the apartment.

- [ ] Go on a road trip together and explore a new city.

- [ ] Decorate the apartment for an international holiday theme.

- [ ] Go on a double date with one roommate and two strangers.

- [ ] Make an apero with wine, cheese, meat cuts, and appetizers.

- [ ] Stay up all night drinking and having deep conversations.

- [ ] Celebrate a roommate's birthday in a big way.

- [ ] Make a roommate photo wall where you can post captured events in the apartment with a notepad section.

- [ ] Give each other a personal gift at the end of the experience.

- [ ] Have the perfect Sunday brunch in pajamas all together.

Case Study *(Finding an Apartment)*

Looking for a new room, a new apartment, your first condo or house and even looking for an accommodation for your next big trip is something that will come often in your global citizen life. Take this opportunity to build the right habits, find the right tools, and build your own techniques.

PERSONA:	Qiao Nie :: 24 years old :: China Exchange city: Paris, France University: Paris-Dauphine
PROBLEM:	It's her first time out of her parents' home and her country. She doesn't speak French and has no contacts in Paris to help her find a room.
SITUATION:	With this problem on hand, her parents decided to help her find the perfect room so she can be safe and at the same time focus on her studies. They opted to forego of cheaper options they saw online. They looked instead for a student residence and an agency that offered personal care services.

ACTION PLAN CONT:	After researching, calling and exchanging emails with both options, they came up with this analysis. Comparing Pros and Cons of the La Cité Internationale Universitaire de Paris Comparing Pros and Cons of booking on Uniplaces a room near her university Here's the resources they've used to validate their comparaisons. • https://erasmusu.com/ • https://www.trustpilot.com/review/uniplaces.com • https://www.residenceetudiante.fr • https://www.uniplaces.com/ • https://www.fac-habitat.com/ • https://www.studapart.com/en • https://fr.airbnb.com/s/Paris--France/ • https://www.campusfrance.org/ • http://www.ciup.fr/
RESULTS:	They ended up deciding that it's better for Qiao Nie to stay in La Cité Internationale Universitaire de Paris to have strong contacts with international students from around the world and also benefit from the residence community activities. They believe it will help her a lot to integrate, especially in a foreign country with a language she doesn't speak.
WISDOM:	Finding the right accommodation could be very exhausting and challenging no matter the situation. From the moment you start to look for it, it would seem like a full time job that could take 1-2 weeks. But in the end, finding the right place can change everything. Your new home could drain all your energy or boost you with bliss. Send the right vibration and vision, the right place will be served by the universe.

3 - PRACTICAL TIPS
All the apps and tricks to use

Finding great wifi:
- Make sure your apartment has 20+mbps to support all the roommates streaming. Use the Speedtest App.
- Find yourself a good coffee shop with strong wifi with great working tables or coworking places where you can pay per day or per hour to go pull up productive work. Check coworkers.com
- Check out if the university library has 20+mbps
- Use a phone app for wifi map finder to find places to pull up quick work sessions on the go

Sim Card & phone number:
- Get a prepaid sim card with 1G of monthly data. Download maps for navigation
- Use the TextNow app to get a free phone number to call and text unlimited via wifi https://www.textnow.com/
- Use Messenger, TextNow, Skype, or WhatsApp calling or voicenote for the rest
- Get an abroad data plan for your first days before buying a local sim card

Grocery stores:
- Get the rewards or points card to save on specific promotions and collect freebies
- Use delivery service to save time and energy like https://www.rappi.com/ or https://www.instacart.com/

Money, ATM, International transfer:
- Open a local bank account. Some banks will give you a 100$ welcome bonus

- Transfer all your semester budget into your local account with https://transferwise.com/ or do a one-time big wire transfer.
- Get a digital bank like https://www.revolut.com/ or https://n26.com/
- Pay your biggest expenses with your PayPal money transferred from your checking account at home. https://www.paypal.com/us/webapps/mpp/what-can-paypal-do

The arrival paper works:
- University course schedule confirmation
- Local medical insurance paperwork
- Verify all your paperwork with the host country immigration office since being illegal can lead the host country to block your entry for the next five years

Events & Social life:
- Create a personal Google Calendar where you put all events you would like to attend the next week
- Search events on global sites like https://www.eventbrite.com/ or https://www.meetup.com/ or https://www.facebook.com/local/
- Find festival tickets https://www.festicket.com/
- World's best festival experiences https://www.cntraveller.com/gallery/best-festivals
- Search Airbnb Experiences and Trip Advisors activities

Restaurants apps:
- Local blogs or news website blogging about the Top Things list. (Example: Narcity, Timeout)
- https://www.opentable.com
- https://www.rappi.com/
- https://eatigo.com/

Travel gear to study abroad:
- Global transformer plug adapter
- Laundry bag
- Net bags or any kind of compartment bags to classify your stuff per categories
- Flip flop for the hostel showers
- Small dose of laundry detergent, deodorant and toothpaste in case of emergencies
- Inflatable travel pillow, foam earplugs, and eye cover for nights on the road
- A folding water bottle
- A small backpack for your weekend trips
- A field note and a pen to list down your best thoughts
- A small umbrella, rain jacket, or raincoat for wet weather
- A USB flash drive to save your big file photos and videos
- A portable phone battery pack
- A waterproof phone case to take photos of your sea expeditions
- A padlock for the hostel or swimming pool lockers

Book tours:
- https://www.tourradar.com/
- https://airbnb.com/host/experiences
- Search free walking tours like https://www.neweuropetours.eu/
- https://www.viator.com/
- https://www.tripadvisor.com/

Download travel apps:
- https://www.hopper.com/
- https://www.skyscanner.net/
- https://fr.airbnb.com/
- https://www.speedtest.net/apps

- https://www.tripadvisor.com/
- https://www.polarsteps.com/ or https://esplor.io/

Download local transportation apps:
- https://www.uber.com/
  https://www.busbud.com
- https://www.wanderu.com
- https://transitapp.com/ or country-related public transportation app
- https://www.waze.com/ if you are renting a car
- https://maps.me/ or Google Map offline

4 - THE CULTURE SHOCK
I want to go back home

Don't feel ashamed that it happens to you; everyone passed through it. It's part of the roller coaster experience. It starts after the third or fourth day and slowly fades in after one or two weeks. The cultural shock is basically home sickness due to the over-whelming amount of adaptation challenging experiences coming in all at once. You'll realize that you are in that phase when you tend to stay in your room too much avoiding the real world. You'll feel loneliness and sadness. If this continues on a few days, you'll tend to feel mild depression.

Here's a step-by-step guide to get out of it as fast as possible. Remember, if you can be conscious about your emotional states, get out of dark thoughts and beat the cycle, you'll build yourself a strong skill for life.

Steps to get out of the cultural shock fast:

- ☐ As fast as possible, find your exchange semester comfortable homie room you'll stay in.

- ☐ Call your parents and family often.

- ☐ Go out every night meeting new people.

- ☐ Smile at everyone you encounter on the street.

- ☐ Do sports every day to overcome these thoughts.

- ☐ Meditate five minutes a day to find home inside you.

- ☐ Be genuinely interested in people's stories listening deeply for true connection.

- ☐ Create your core crew of 5–6 friends.

My Story on the Topic...

I realized I was in the cultural shock when one night I crumbled whilst trying to fall asleep. I was thinking of everything that has been happening and ended up telling myself that all those bad lucks meant this experience was just not for me. I started crying, and one night, I called my mom. Never in a thousand years would I cry calling my mom to relieve my pain, it is just not the way I've been raised. It was just all the accumulation of the little things that I kept inside that led to this explosive moment. Getting lost at arrival from the airport to the apartment of Anne, I've asked people in the streets for help to be surprised by the fact that no one was speaking English. All the housing-hunting troubles where I had to call the apartment tenant one by one to see if the room was still available and if I could come visit.

That was before the age of smartphones, common use of rooms marketplace, or Facebook groups. Most of the ads I was calling were from the school billboard or from walking down the street and stumbling on one apartment announcement. All those ads were outdated and most of the tenants didn't speak English.

Little moments added up like the time I went to a coffee shop with Anne and her boyfriend, we all ordered paninis which the Italian coffee tenant do one by one while serving the counter which took a bit of time. When I finally received my panini, I took it in my hand and realized that the hidden side was completely burnt. So I asked Anne's Italian boyfriend if that was normal. He then took it to the coffee tenant to ask why he did that and his response was that he thought I was French, from France, and he didn't like French people.

A lot of little situations like that happened where Italian were not really welcoming, didn't speak English, and didn't want to help. All those little accumulation plus my indefinite room-hunting and the fact that I was starting to take too much place at Anne's apartment, led me to my breakdown.

5 - SPIRITUALITY
How to face loneliness

Stuck in a world of constant attention seekers, it is so easy to avoid our responsibilities and our personal inner problems. Learn how to satisfy your own happiness like you were living on a desert island.

Make meditation part of your life.

Meditation is the ultimate daily practice that can solve a thousand problems. Don't be too harsh on yourself; it takes time to be good at it and fully understand its super powers. You will need a minimum of 200+ hours to even start understanding some small potential effects on your daily life.

Here's a list of the main benefits:
- Decreases depression
- Helps regulate mood and anxiety disorders
- Reduces stress
- Controls anxiety
- Promotes emotional health
- Enhances self-awareness
- Lengthens attention span
- May reduce age-related memory loss
- Can generate kindness
- May help fight addictions
- Improves sleep
- Helps control pain
- Mindfulness meditation fosters creativity
- Long-term meditation enhances the ability to generate gamma waves in the brain
- Improves information processing and decision-making
- Relieves pain better than morphine
- Improves learning and memory
- Prevents you from falling in the trap of multitasking too often Meditation reduces blood pressure
- Helps prevent asthma, rheumatoid arthritis, and inflammatory bowel disease
- Reduces risk of Alzheimer's and premature death
- Helps manage the heart rate and respiratory rate
- May make you live longer
- Loving-kindness meditation improves empathy and positive relationships
- Loving-kindness meditation also reduces social isolation
- Reduces emotional eating

There are nine stages of meditation mind training of mahamudra or great imprint:
1. The meditator is like a rocky boat in a turbulent ocean. There's virtually no control on the mind. The concentration at this stage ends up wherever the drift of thoughts take it.
2. It shows progress. It means the meditator is able to have short periods of quality meditation when the mind is devoid of thoughts. Think of a flag that flutters whenever the wind blows. No wind, no fluttering. Similarly, the mind at this stage is stable for a short period before the winds of thoughts start to blow again causing waves in the stillness of consciousness.
3. We are able to detect dullness arising in meditation. Restlessness or stray thoughts are still a great challenge at this stage.
4.&5.While the meditator makes a giant leap with greater taming of restlessness and dullness, a new challenge presents itself. A state of calmness which makes the meditator go into a sort of lethargy. Often, most meditators, who get even a tiny glimpse of this calmness, mistake this as the ultimate state of bliss.
6. The meditator has mostly tamed the body, mind, and distractions, he's able to lead them, but there are still subtle elements of excitement or stupor that can distract the meditator.
7. The meditator has nearly perfected the art of attention. They experience lucid awareness during the meditation, but there's still a chance of feeling excited or restless. Think of a still pond where dropping even a tiny pebble causes ripples.
8. Restlessness has completely disappeared for this meditator and a constant state of bliss always leaves them calm.

But, sometimes in this state of bliss, the lucidity of their awareness is adversely affected. Think of someone under the influence of a mild intoxicant. At this stage, the meditator hasn't yet learned to rise above the bliss.

9. Bliss has become a close companion and it no longer interferes in any worldly activity. All mental and emotional battles cease, the war of thoughts stops, and there's virtually no effort in meditation now. The meditator has become the meditation.

To achieve maximum results, you need to physically use those meditation tricks:

- Sit on the floor to be grounded with your Root Chakra, the red light energy connecting you to mother earth. The Root Chakra is linked to the foundation in which we base our lives: security, safety, survival, basic needs (food, sleep, shelter, self-preservation, etc.), physical identity, aspects of self and grounding.
- Have your back straight, shoulder and chest strong, spine vertically straight
- Put the tip of your tongue behind your upper teeth, removing your tongue from the top of your mouth will relax all your face muscles and your jaw
- Have an inner smile with the left and right tip of your lips turning up a bit
- Sit in half lotus or full lotus to not block the blood circulation in the feet touching the ground
- Put your hands on your lap facing up towards the universe while connecting the tip of your thumb with your index finger together and keep the three other fingers stretched and relaxed. This is the Gyan (or Chin) mudra, a gesture that facilitates the flow of energy in the subtle body. The

intention is to improve concentration, creativity, sharpen your memory, and gain knowledge.

- Keep your chin tucked in slightly while maintaining length in the back of your neck. Correctly positioning your chin helps you to maintain your posture. Keep your face relaxed. You may find that turning the corners of your face up slightly helps to release any tension in the face.
- Avoid squeezing your eyes shut. Softly closing them will help you keep your face, eyes, and eyelids relaxed.

There are many types of meditation focusing on different intentions. Here are the main ones:

- **Loving Kindness Meditation.** Simple practice of directing well wishes towards other people
- **Body scan or progressive relaxation.** You mentally "scan" your muscles looking for areas of tension. Whenever you discover an area of tension, gently move the muscle to loosen it, and then relax it.
- **Mindfulness meditation.** A mental training practice that involves focusing your mind on your experiences (like your own emotions, thoughts, and sensations) in the present moment
- **Breath awareness meditation.** Practice giving full awareness to the breath
- **Tonglen Meditation.** A traditional Buddhist meditation often referred to as "taking and sending," in which we take in the pain of the world with our inhalation, and breathe out our own comfort, healing, and goodness.
- **Kundalini yoga.** A magical science that uses sound, mantra, energy healing, exercises, and meditations to release trauma from the energetic body, which surrounds the physical body.

- **Zen meditation.** Zen is a Japanese school of Mahayana Buddhism. The purpose of meditation is to stop the mind rushing about in an aimless (or even a purposeful) stream of thoughts.
- **Transcendental Meditation.** A form of silent mantra meditation, developed by Maharishi Mahesh Yogi. The meditation practice involves the use of a mantra and is practiced for 20 minutes twice per day.
- **Vipassana Meditation.** Vipassana can be translated as "Insight," a clear awareness of exactly what is happening as it happens. Samatha can be translated as "concentration" or "tranquility." It is a state in which the mind is brought to rest, focused only on one item and not allowed to wander. When this is done, a deep calm pervades body and mind, a state of tranquility which must be experienced to be understood. Most systems of meditation emphasize the Samatha component.
- **Guided Meditation.** Guided meditation is a process by which one or more participants meditate in response to the guidance provided by a trained practitioner or teacher, either in person or via a written text, sound recording, video, or audiovisual media comprising music or verbal instruction, or a combination of both.
- **Taoist Emptiness meditation.** Also spelled "Daoist", it refers to the traditional meditative practices associated with the Chinese philosophy and religion of Taoism, including concentration, mindfulness, contemplation, and visualization

5 Categories of Brain Waves to Access Deep Meditation:
Slower wavelengths = more time between thoughts = more opportunity to skillfully choose which thoughts you invest in and what actions you take.

1. **Gamma State:** (30–100Hz) This is the state of hyper-activity and active learning. Gamma state is the most opportune time to retain information.
2. **Beta State:** (13–30Hz) Where we function for most of the day, Beta State is associated with the alert mind state of the prefrontal cortex. This is a state of the "working" or "thinking mind": analytical, planning, assessing and categorizing.
3. **Alpha State:** (9–13Hz) Brain waves start to slow down out of thinking mind. We feel more calm, peaceful, and grounded. We often find ourselves in an "alpha state" after a yoga class, a walk in the woods, pleasurable sexual encounter, or during any activity that helps relax the body and mind.
4. **Theta State:** (4–8Hz) We're able to begin meditation. This is the point where the verbal/thinking mind transitions to the meditative/visual mind. We begin to move from the planning mind to a deeper state of awareness (often felt as drowsy), with stronger intuition, more capacity for wholeness and complicated problem solving. The Theta state is associated with visualization.
5. **Delta State:** (1–3 Hz) Tibetan monks who have been meditating for decades can reach this in an alert, wakened phase, but most of us reach this final state during deep, dreamless sleep.

Tips for beginners:
- Start with shorter practices and increase as you feel comfortable.
- Your first milestone is to do 12 minutes of concentration meditation, then 24 minutes.
- Focus on your breath moving in and out through your body.
- Keep your breath slow, steady, and smooth.

- Observe all thoughts, feelings, and sensations as they arise and pass. Remember that these can be positive, negative, and neutral.
- Gently bring your mind back to the present without judgment when it wanders.
- Be conscious of the silence and stillness within.
- Bring your awareness to the sounds around you one by one.
- Feel the air or clothing touching your skin and feel your body touching the floor.

Do 3–5 immersive experiences per year.

The best way to grow in life is to take massive in-field action pushing yourself out of your comfort zone. 4–5 times a year, block yourself 5–10 days to fully immerse yourself in an experience that pushes your understanding of your mind, soul, and the universe.

Vipassana. A ten-day silent retreat with zero mind distraction (no music, reading, journaling, talking, sports, smiling at others, etc.) and ten hours of meditation a day while waking up at 4 am and eating only vegetarian.

Ayahuasca. Considered to be one of the most popular types of plant medicine giving you access to your subconscious, the 5th dimension of the spirit world and the answer you were looking for. Other popular plant medicines are the San Pedro Cactus, Peyote, and Peruvian Torch Cactus

Be a Monk for 1 to 3 Months. Fully disconnect from modern society chaos of money machine and technology. Immerse yourself deeply with the experts of the mind.

Ten-day Dark Room Retreat. After 300+ hours in total darkness with zero distraction, your brain starts releasing naturally Dimethyltryptamine or DMT, emerging yourself into the spirit world.

Wim Hof Extreme Cold Exposure. How to control your body and mind for self-healing and strength.

Hell Week of the Navy Seals. Famously the hardest thing a human can go through physically. You can now do the commercial version of it with Sealfit.

Digital Detox. Disconnect to go back to what really matters and have more awareness of your internet and television use in order to gain more control of your life.

Festivals. There are some immersive festival experiences that get you feeling like you landed on another planet, such as the world-famous Burning Man, in the desert of Nevada.

Peregrinaje. The most famous one is the El Camino de Santiago in the north of Spain with more than 800 km of walking to do in 30+ days by yourself. Watch the movie, *The Way*, to sense the expedition. Also, take a look at multi-site pilgrimage of 88 temples associated with the Buddhist monk Kūkai on the island of Shikoku, Japan.

Yoga Retreat. Mastering the mind-body, the inter-relationship between one's physical health, and the state of one's mind or spirit.

Trekking a mega mountain. Himalaya, Kathmandu, or why not Mount Everest, trekking the world's highest peaks will push every piece of the body and mental strength you have.

Meditation Retreat. Meditation, a transcendental practice, is coming out of the temple to the day-to-day western world slowly moving to be practiced by the majority of us. There are many types of meditations, providing all kinds of benefits.

Marathon des Sables. Known as the toughest foot race in the world. A marathon of 6 days through 251km in the Sahara desert.

Fasting (Water or Dry Fasting). Three days of water fasting 3–4 times a year could give you an extra 20 years of longevity

Ecstatic Dance. Close your eyes and let your body flow to the music like no one is watching. Biodanza (the dance of life) is also to be considered.

Tantric Sex (Neotantra). Relearn everything you think you knew about sex.

Hypnotherapy. All the answers are inside you. Accept your sub-conscious mind to bring back memories of why you have specific self-destruction behavior.

Búsqueda de Visión (Vision Quest). A vision quest is a rite of passage in some Native American cultures. The process includes a complete fast for four days and nights, alone at a sacred site in nature. You are partnered with a soul mate that stays in the village while supporting you mentally through his/her meditation and positive vibration.

Smoking DMT or Toad Venom 5 MeO DMT (illegal in some countries). Smoking DMT gives you an 8–10-minute intense out-of-body experience letting you understand the boundaries of our physical world with the 5th dimension, the spirit world. After, you have a sense of an ego death, body form death, and mind death. You won't be scared of dying anymore because you'll understand what is after this life.

Temazcal. 2–3 hours in a natural sauna where four cycles of different chanting are done to heal your past and future. It represents the womb, and people coming out of the bath are, in a symbolic sense, re-born.

Iboga. Iboga stimulates the central nervous system when taken in small doses and induces hallucinations in larger doses. In parts of Africa where the plant grows, the bark of the root is chewed for various pharmacological or ritualistic purposes.

Kambô. Kambo is a traditional ritual that uses the poison of the giant monkey frog, to purify the body and treat various health conditions.

*For resources and awesome YouTube videos on each experience above, go to jfbrou.com and find the article on 22 life experiences that will make you meet your soul.

6 - MASTERING SOCIAL DYNAMICS
Be socially bold connecting with new humans

Some people are born socially bold, but for the rest of us it is a never-ending struggle. This is the ultimate soft skill no one teaches you about. Like every new skill, the goal is to practice, to repeat, and to be persistent over time to become great at it. And when the day comes that you become great at this, it will open great opportunities for you, a pandora box of contacts, experiences, and resources.

How to break the ice with anyone in the street or at an event:
- **Wear a conversation starter.** Wearing something a little unique and beautiful can drag attention and have people open up to you about it and then you transition by complimenting them.
- **Play the Beginner.** "Excuse me, I just felt like talking to you." Sometimes the best and most fun icebreaker is honesty.
- **Accept the risk of rejection and being awkward.** Obviously, not everyone will accept your good energy. Most people are stuck in their own head filled with to-dos and worries. Don't take it personally; they were not just on the same energy vibe as yours.
- **Ask them about themselves.** Everyone LOVES talking about themselves; give them an opportunity to express the deepest human being need.
- **Asking an open-ended question.** Never ask questions that could end with "yes" or "no". Always ask questions with How, What, Why, When to have them opening up on a subject. When they think they are finished with their answer, ask, "Why? Can you tell more about X?" to have them dig deeper.

- **Know their names.** This is SO important. Here are some tips below:
    - Remembering names of people is BIG, here's the trick[2]:
    - Know your motivation. Motivation is the force that drives memory. Why you want to remember names of people? (For your network, friends, love, etc.)
    - Focus on the person you are talking to. You don't stand a chance of remembering a new name if you are daydreaming about your weekend plans. Give your utmost attention.
    - Repeat the name of the person you just met. One way to help you remember a person's name is to find a way to repeat it right after you first learned it.
    - Focus on a particular feature of the person's face. Pick out a facial feature that may be easy to remember. Search for the most distinguishing feature, whether it is a small nose, large ears, unusual hairdo, or deep dimples. Connecting a name to a visual trait helps anchor the name in your memory
    - Link the new name with something you already know. Connecting a new name to a person or object that is already stored in your memory is another way to anchor a new name in your memory.
    - Break down complicated names with mnemonic devices.For complex names, ask the person to spell the name and visualize the spelling.
    - Repeat a new name when you say goodbye. Each time you repeat a new name, it helps. People will like you more than others by calling them by their names.

---

2   https://www.cnbc.com/2016/09/21/11-memory-hacks-to-remember-the-names-of-everyone-you-meet.html

- Go back over the names you knew at the end of a day. After events or networking events, go back through your top persons list, recall their names, and note them on your database.

Keep in mind the future and start networking:
- **Know your goals and have a vision.** Know yourself perfectly and where you are going in life. Do the *Become Your Best Version* workbook, resume in the Appendix section and sold on Amazon.
- **Have a database system.** Have a system to take contacts. Facebook or Instagram for friends, LinkedIn for professional contacts, WhatsApp or Phone numbers in case a call maybe needed
- **Classify people per expertise and resource.** From all your data entries, extract them all in one spreadsheet to then classify people by topic, resources, skills, etc. Everything you can to identify what you are looking for in the future and be connected with potential opportunity linking a step closer to your vision.

Creating connections in group conversation with new people.
- **Intent and freedom from outcome.** Make sure you know what your intention is before going in a group conversation. What are you trying to get out of it? Do not have too high expectations to not be disappointed of the outcome. Trying your best is the prize, a step towards your better self.
- **Social momentum.** You are more inclined to have fluid conversational energy in a group when you are mentally strong. You need to build yourself into the right momentum. Talking to other people before, meditating, stretching, whatever that builds you into having strong awareness and brings you to a state of joy.

- **Being totally present.** Don't daydream or have your mind
  wander with questions, just be fully present in the moment.
  Active listening with your body or facial response is your
  goal. Smile and give your full attention.
- **Circle back personally on the thing that touched you.**
  Once the group conversation has ended, right after or later
  that day, contact one person from the group to express
  your gratitude for the conversation telling him or her that
  you really related to what he/she said.

7 - THE ORGANIZATION THAT WILL CHANGE EVERYTHING
OKAY!!!! This is it

What really makes or break an incredible exchange semester
is the fact that there's an organization or students association in
your abroad destination that satisfies the social life of exchange
students. It's this small and strong community aspect with all the
200–400 exchange students of your university that really makes
it a unique experience. Bonding with the same people that you
encounter at every party, trip, classroom, and social gathering creates life-changing peripeties that everyone in this community love
to share or gossip about.

Here's the list of the top exchange students organizations in
the world:
- https://interstude.com/
- http://baisargentina.com/
- https://www.integratemexico.com/
- https://santiagoexchange.com/
- http://www.conexionmexico.com.mx/

- https://erasmuslifelisboa.com/
- http://www.esn.org/
- http://www.reirio.org/
- https://www.tobeerasmusinparis.com/
- https://erasmusbarcelona.com/
- https://www.isx.ca/

Erasmus gathering events:
- https://erasmusnation.com/
- https://esnibizatrip.org/
- https://www.facebook.com/ESNseabattle/

Erasmus registry:
- http://exchangeyourlife.org
- https://erasmusu.com/

Also, be on the lookout for private Facebook groups and students association via Facebook researches with the keywords "Erasmus", "Exchange Students", "International Students", "Expats", and "PVTiste".

The best thing you could do to maximize your exchange is to assist one of those organizations welcome gathering to make sure that you meet the most exchange on the day that no one knows each other. Don't be shy and stick around with your roommates or people of the same country. Break your comfort zone by going to people. Say hi, smile, *my name is*...and everyone will be the most welcoming.

KEYNOTES SUMMARY OF THE CHAPTER:

- The present moment is the only thing we have, be there with your child's mind.

- Finding the right accommodation is what is going to change everything, don't mess it up.

- Explore all the tips and apps to support you through the journey.

- You can beat the culture shock; control your mind, don't let it control you.

- The spiritual journey will fix all your other wheel of life dimensions, jump on it now.

- Patterns are everywhere, practice how to analyze social dynamics to then feel more comfortable with approaching new people.

- Find the organization that will maximize your exchange.

NEXT CHAPTER...

Next chapter, the journey at your destination, you'll feel deeply alive! Are you ready? It's going to pass so fast. No worries, I have the best tips to make the most of your stay.

EXPERT
INTERVIEW :: Diego Larre

https://www.linkedin.com/in/diego-larre-90145322/

How did you get started? I studied Marketing and then neuroscience. Now, I do clinical hypnosis. Everything started from me going to work and studying English in Colorado, United States, at 24 years old, then I went abroad to Europe to travel then I just wanted to gather with the internationals at his university.

With a friend, I started doing parties for them that led to doing trips and meeting many international students. I loved managing the trips and my friend was managing the nights out. At first, it was just for fun, but then the school asked us to create an outside entity, so we created an NGO. From that nonprofit, I created many companies that I stopped or sold, but now I'm still managing three companies that I'm able to live out of. https://timeforargentina.com/

Founder of BAIS Argentina http://baisargentina.com/es

Founded in 2005, an NGO now present in Buenos Aires with presence in Madrid, Puerto Rico, London, Mexico. In Buenos Aires, they are 30+ working full time to integrate the international students.

Most popular nationality going to Buenos Aires are French, Mexicans, and a lot of Brazilians coming to study medicine

We offer traveling, party, social activities, support with housing. Our most popular trip is Iguazu Falls gathering more than 400 students and the welcome party bringing 3000+ students.

THE ERASMUS MARKET

What is your best advice to survive the cultural shock?

1. Go see the organization for exchange students in your city or university
2. Go to the international office desk of our university to ask who went to your city exchange to ask to be in contact with.
3. Do a lot of web research on this city, country, and the culture
4. Find an accommodation near your social life that will be seven days a week. Sometimes there's no social life near the university and you'll have to go there only 3–4 days a week. Where and with who you'll live is the most important step of the semester that will affect everything.

Are you advising students to go live in a student residence or to find a flatshare? Here in Argentina, I recommend finding an apartment because the student residences are very strict. You can't invite friends or make noise; they have a lot of rules. Sometimes they only have common kitchen where it's more complicated to cook freely.

In the past, I've done some studies and we realized that people living in an apartment were happier than people living in a student residence. But I did meet a lot of people that lived in student residences during their exchange and they loved it because they were living with more than 100 exchange students in the same building, so there were always gatherings.

Do you advise students to book their apartment before arriving? In Argentina, you can't trust the pictures. So it's better to do your research, create yourself a wish list, and coordinate with the owner to go visit them on your first week when you arrive.

Do you have any exchange student's story gone bad? Yes, some students died during their exchange because they rented a car and they were driving fast while drinking and being distracted.

What is your advice to keep in touch with your family during your exchange? For almost all South Americans in exchange in Buenos Aires, one member of their family comes to visit them. It's an excuse to travel. For European, if they have a boyfriend or girlfriend, they will come, but the parents, not really.

Why do you think there are people that don't want to go on exchange? For most of them it's because of the money; it's not easy for most South Americans to afford to live for six months in another country. Also, a lot of people just don't know about the opportunity, as it is not well advertised in the universities.

What are the top professional skills that the exchange students get from this experience? First of all, it opens their mind. They realize that what they saw in the news about this culture or country is not the real situation. And, obviously, they get a lot of love and friends; friends are the most important thing.

Now, you have friends around the world that you can trust, for example, if you need to open a new business or travel to that country. A lot of exchange students use their network like that to then travel the world without spending much, being hosted for free. And for my business, I prefer to work with people that travel; they are more autodidact in their work.

What are is best advice to beat the post-Erasmus depression? Join an organization that welcomes foreign people in your country. Give back what you received.

What is your best travel tip? Try to live with the people of the country. For example, if you go to Cancun and stay at the hotel, you are a tourist, but if you go to Michoacan and stay in a local family house, a part of you becomes Mexican.

THE ENTREPRENEURSHIP MINDSET

What has been the most challenging situation in business for you? I have challenges every day because I start a new project or I need to motivate my team. But my biggest challenge was to start BAIS Argentina with no money and giving no salary for the first five years. And also, it's very hard to be NGO in Argentina; the government is a real pain.

What did you wish you knew about business? How to structure the organization properly and delegate to the right people so that I don't end up doing everything by myself for so long.

Do you think entrepreneurs are born or made? I think you need to be born and made, because you have to fail and learn a lot.

Is there anyone that inspires you? My dad inspires me to be brave and never give up.

Is there a book that you suggest to the next generation? *Jonathan Livingston Seagull* by Richard Bach

CONCLUSION

Happiness is...smiling.

Life is...happiness.

An exchange student is...free

Entrepreneurship is...brave

The greatest pleasure in life is...to help.

The best thing I ever did was...to love.

A good traveler is...a person that can dream it and make it happen.

CHAPTER 4

The Exchange

IT WILL PASS SO FAST

1 - LIVING IN EXCHANGE
How to have an incredible experience

If you don't know how to fully live an exchange abroad, you'll never know how to fully live a life, that's for sure. Going abroad means living its uniqueness among equally unique students from all over the world. And it is these human differences that allow everyone to appreciate the experience. Everyone is somewhat exotic! Everyone is someone! At one's joke, they will laugh at you wondering if you are from Mars because your English accent is different from anyone else's. At this point, you become the ambassador of your city, state, country, and most especially your culture. When there's a random question in the air about your country or city, you become the go-to expert. When there's a global breaking news from your country, everyone will ask about this subject when they meet you. And finally, some ask you to cook them your national dish.

HERE'S YOUR BUCKET LIST TO MAKE THE MOST OF YOUR EXCHANGE EXPERIENCE:

- ☐ Learn the basics of a new language.
- ☐ Go on a road trip.
- ☐ Go on a bus tour weekend trip.
- ☐ Go to a festival with your international friends.
- ☐ Party 'til morning.
- ☐ Do an international cuisine potluck.
- ☐ Party for four nights straight.
- ☐ Do a cremaillere housewarming party at your apartment.
- ☐ Do a free walking tour of your host city.
- ☐ Try the top three bars of your host city.
- ☐ Try the top three restaurants of your host city.
- ☐ Try the top three clubs of your host city.
- ☐ Try the top three tourist activities of your host city.
- ☐ Try an Airbnb experience of your host city.
- ☐ Do a weekend in a cottage outside the city with your international friends.
- ☐ Go volunteering for a full day.
- ☐ Be an ambassador of your country for an organization or one big event.
- ☐ Convince your parents and siblings to come visit you.

- [ ] Fall in love with a local.

- [ ] Go to a local comedy show.

- [ ] Pass the afternoon hanging out in the most beautiful park of the city.

- [ ] Join a social group class or club of your host university.

- [ ] Experiment potential passions.

- [ ] Go to the cinema to watch a movie with the local language with English sub-title.

- [ ] Taste all the famous local food.

- [ ] Do a video souvenir of all your exchange.

- [ ] Cook your national dish for your best friends.

- [ ] Go experience a local mega sports event.

- [ ] Go hunt the most breathtaking views of the city.

- [ ] Go on a water or beach party trip.

- [ ] Watch the movie, *The Spanish Apartment,* during and after your Erasmus.

- [ ] Take a selfie with your professor.

- [ ] Create a memory box of meaningful souvenirs.

- [ ] Go bungee jumping, skydiving, or paragliding pushing your fear of heights.

- [ ] Get a tattoo.

- [ ] Attend the semester welcome weekend of your host university.

- [ ] Write a blog post about a topic of your exchange experience.

Many marketing content of the exchange program have boosted the trend over the years. Here are some examples:

1.   ERASMUS 30 YEARS
2.   We Are One - Experience the Erasmus Generation
3.   Studying Abroad - Why You Should Do It! (Full Length)

2 - THE DON'TS
How to live a real nightmare

Definitely not only success stories come with the exchange experience. Definitely not everyone ended up with the spirit "Erasmus one day, Erasmus forever". But to be honest, I think it's their own fault; it's their conditioning from the very beginning. Experiences come from within. It comes from your state of mind, inner peace, thoughts monitoring. Two people could be living the exact totally normal experience, for example, but for one person it could be such a grateful experience of human connection, a special moment in his lifetime, while for another person it could be just a normal experience, he could be thinking it's slightly overpriced and that the entire experience can be improved. On top of your state of mind, there are definitely some situations to avoid at all costs.

First one by far is leaving a girlfriend/boyfriend at home while you fly away to live the experience of your life. This shall occupy much of your thoughts and attention, thinking of her/him, thinking of calling/texting her/him while you are out with fellow exchange. Don't get me wrong here, I understand that love is something that is very hard to get out of your head. It takes months to pass to another stage in your life and fully stop thinking about the person. So maybe this is something you should think ahead before leaving on exchange. Have that conversation with your girlfriend/boyfriend.

Second one is to hang out mostly with people of your nationality. This is a big mistake that a lot of people make; they can't fight the out-of-comfort zone feeling and they directly go about with what they know. But when you do this from the beginning, you enter a rabbit hole that is extremely difficult to get out of. Because those people will like the same feeling of comfort, it's going to be very difficult to get out of the addiction of not being alone. One of the best skills you could build is to satisfy yourself with your own solitude, with personal passions and worthwhile experiences you do alone.

Third one would be to spend most of your money on the first month. I got it, for the first time in life you have this wild budget and you get caught in this exciting moment like it's the honeymoon period of a new lifestyle. This was my biggest mistake in Milan; I literally spent 50% of my entire exchange budget in the first month. Don't ask me how, I still don't know how that money went away so fast. I paid the price of it at the end of my exchange the hard way where I ended up stuck on the Greek island Ios and worked under the table for 30€ a day while eating a 2€ gyros for every meal.

Forth one would be to trust a bad apartment tenant. They will be draining all your energy all the time. There are a lot of small business owners out there in the rooming industry trying to exploit international students. They know you wouldn't sue them from the difficulties they have caused you from another country. There are a lot of stories out there, asking of deposits that you'll never see again, overcharging random fees, entering the apartment without notice invading your private space, being unavailable to fix apartment issues and the list goes on.

Last one on my list to not do during your exchange is to fall in love unless you know it's the one. Again, I know that this is easier said than done. But if that happens, be ready for extremely challenging post-Erasmus depression.

Here's a list of common cultural things you should know to not offend local people when abroad:
- Be aware of the tipping policies
- Have some manners at the restaurants
- Know the basics of the language
- Learn the don'ts of specific countries. Examples: Don't eat with your left hand in India, don't hug people in Korea

Most common travel mistakes you shouldn't do:
- Packing too much
- Not having a spare phone battery back and phone charger in your carry-on
- Not having an eye mask, earplugs, and inflatable pillow
- Not having security tools like a padlock for the hostel, public pool, or festival
- Not researching ahead. Do your research prior and plan to experience the history of the location, culinary, modern trendy place and be adventurous going out of your comfort zone.
- Not securing a travel insurance
- Not having a travel credit card like Revolut or N26 to not pay the 2.5% exchange fee on each transaction
- Not having international internet data on your phone to solve any problems
- Checking in late at the airport. Check in at least 1h30 to not miss your flight and what's even better is to check in as soon as you can in the 24h before your flight so you don't get the last worst seat available
- Having a black luggage and backpack looking like everyone else's. Have something on it that will make it stand out so it won't be mistaken as another's

3 - DISCOVERING A NEW CULTURE
The wonders

Jumping in deep into the culture of your exchange destination is like falling in love at first sight. Suddenly, you find yourself passionately interested in this thing you know nothing about. Then you discover it over time, peeling layer after layer, and each discovery will seem like a cherry blossom blooming, a wonder that will for the longest time, if not a lifetime, leave you in awe. On your journey back home, you shall carry this second nationality, a bond of belonging that you will cherish for life.

It's not only the culture of your destination country that will leave a mark on you, but also the best manners, ideas, and customs of the culture of your best exchange friends leaving you with an arsenal of tools that will make you into a global citizen.

Here's the simple-to-say-but-harder-to-constantly-do trick to fully imprint yourself with other cultures: embrace your child's mind, keep your eyes right open and listen 90% of the time.

DISCOVERING NEW CULTURE TIPS:

- ☐ Do your own deep research about your host country culture on YouTube or read on different topics: politics, history, comparing regions, education system, social system, etc.

- ☐ Open your eyes like a child's, listen actively, and connect with your heart.

- ☐ Understand that what might be rude for you is totally normal for them. We all have different cultural upbringings embed into deep habits.

- ☐ Avoid imposing your own values.

- ☐ Don't stereotype and put all the country's people in the same box.

- ☐ Accept your own naivety.

- ☐ Learn a new language.

- ☐ Learn new skills strongly embed into their culture.

- ☐ Watch local TV series & movies with subtitles.

- ☐ Listen to local music from different genres.

- ☐ Search their most famous artists who left a huge impact on their culture.

- ☐ Try their best tradition dishes.

- ☐ Do cultural experiences.

- ☐ Travel around the country.

4 - THE FIRST TIMES
There are so much of them in exchange

Your first flatshare is your first personal home you will be nostalgic about with all those silly, unconventional, old or broken things you lived with.

Your first grocery shopping will last three hours of walking slowly, alley per alley, while picking up and analyzing each product amazed by its difference from what's usual in your country.

Your first national dish will be the most mindful meal of your life; you'll be tasting every bit and eating slowly like your parents always told you to do so.

Your first date will be full of awkward moments leading to most likely awkward sex on a first date.

Your first exchange student party will be the party you'll meet the most people in your life.

Your first exchange student trip will be the most unorganized freestyle trip of your life leading you to a lot of unexpected discoveries.

Your first class will leave you speechless on how the teacher is having strange manners and how different the students are reacting to the class.

Your first exam will be challenging not because of the content, but of how questions are framed, making you think twice, that you'll be the last to finish the exam.

HOW TO FULLY LIVE ALL FIRST EXPERIENCES:

- ☐ Reduce stress with deep preparation mastering the subject.

- ☐ Calm yourself just before through a quick meditation and deep breathing.

- ☐ Defeat negative self-talk and bring in positive vibrations and self-confidence.

- ☐ Don't have expectations, accept every moment as they are, learning lessons along the way.

- ☐ Don't try to perform into something you are not, just be open with your weaknesses and be yourself as you are now.

- ☐ Slowly start being mindful and embrace the power of now at every breath.

- ☐ Don't compare your experiences with others; everyone lives them differently from his own upbringing and knowledge.

- ☐ Create and keep tangible souvenirs like photos, videos, or other objects.

- ☐ Be deeply grateful for the experience you had with yourself and others.

5 - TRAVEL, TRAVEL
Let's go spend everything in two months

Why do we, humans, explore? We always want to explore for more, to go deeper, to push the boundaries to our limits to truly know what is possible. We explore for the thrill of discovering the unknown, for the adrenaline of the unexpected, for the feeling it gives us to be fully present and alive.

Exploration is an inner discovery of your true potential. In the beginning, you might be motivated by the need to prove something to someone or to yourself, but over time it will become like a constant need and you'll know that you can do anything you put your mind into. Exploration is a skill you'll start learning with your exchange experience; slowly, you'll know the cycle of the journey of the explorer and you'll become a true explorer pushing his comfort zone.

"A SHIP IN HARBOR IS SAFE, BUT THAT IS NOT WHAT SHIPS ARE BUILT FOR."

~ JOHN A. SHEDD

A. BOOKING FLIGHTS
- Research websites: https://www.skyscanner.net/, https://www.google.com/flights, https://www.hopper.com/

- Low cost companies: https://www.ryanair.com, https://www.easyjet.com/, https://www.airasia.com/, https://wowair.com/, https://www.spirit.com/, https://wizzair.com/,

Tips:
- Keep your searches in an incognito browser.
- Identify the cheapest day to fly.
- Fly for free with points.
- Book connecting flights yourself for less.
- Find the cheapest place to fly with Kiwi map or Google flight map.
- Don't forget about local airlines.

B. RENTING A CAR
- Research websites: https://www.kayak.com/cars, https://www.rentalcars.com, https://www.autoeurope.eu/
- Companies: https://www.budget.com, https://www.enterprise.com, https://www.car2go.com/

Tips:
- Get a friend of 25 years and over to save on the insurance cost.
- Use the Kayak car rental for cheaper rate

C. CAR SHARING
- Research websites: https://www.amigoexpress.com/, https://www.poparide.com/, https://www.blablacar.fr/

Tips:
- Reserve 3–5 days in advance.
- Find drivers in your age range

D. TAKING THE TRAIN
- Research websites: https://www.thetrainline.com/, https://www.goeuro.com/, https://www.raileurope.com
- Companies: national companies per country

Tips: Take a multi country train pass if you are in Europe, http://www.railpass.com/

E. TAKING THE BUS

- Research websites: https://www.busbud.com/, https://www.wanderu.com/, https://www.rome2rio.com/
- Companies: https://www.greyhound.com/, https://www.megabus.com/, https://global.flixbus.com/, https://www.boltbus.com/

Tips:

- Book far in advance to get a lower price like 7-day advance purchase (15% off) or 21-day advance purchase (50% off).
- Book through your local hotel/hostel to avoid online aggregator commission fee

F. BOOKING ACCOMMODATION

- Research websites: https://www.hostelworld.com/, https://www.couchsurfing.com/, https://www.agoda.com/, https://www.hotels.com/

Tips: Dorms of 4–6+ beds can be challenging depending on your mood

G. DOING TOURS & EXPERIENCES

- Research websites: https://fr.airbnb.com/s/experiences, https://www.tourradar.com/, https://www.viator.com/, https://www.tripadvisor.com/
- Companies: https://www.neweuropetours.eu/

Tips:

- Check good and bad reviews.
- Read their Terms & Services policies.

H. THE TRAVEL INDUSTRY

- Research websites: https://www.lonelyplanet.com/, https://theculturetrip.com/, https://www.tripsavvy.com/
- Companies: http://www.fctgl.com/, https://ttc.com/, https://skift.com/, https://www.trekksoft.com, https://www.expediagroup.com/

Tips: Follow the top resources on Facebook to be on top of new deals, trends, and insights

I. COFFEE SHOP & RESTAURANTS

- Research websites: https://www.tripadvisor.com/, https://www.yelp.com/

Tips: Search for local mobile apps to get insights on reviews, trends, reservation, and best menu items.

My Story on the Topic...

My first ever road trip. It was my first trip during my exchange in Milan and I can still remember the feeling like it was just yesterday. During my first week in class, I entered my first subject, the class was pretty full and I didn't know anyone just yet. I ended up sitting next to an Indian guy. I didn't cared much about the class, I was in the mindset of meeting as many new people as possible. So I introduced myself to the guy; however, he was a bit cold at first and didn't want to be bothered. But then he opened up and shared that it was his birthday in that coming weekend and he was leaving tomorrow for Rome with some friends with a rental car.

Out of nowhere, without thinking, I asked him, "Wow, can I come with you guys?" He was surprised and wasn't expecting that. He responded, "Ehh, I don't know, maybe, let me ask my friends". By the end of that class, I managed to skip the rest of the week and went on a 5-day road trip to Rome with three other random guys in a tiny two-door Fiat 500 for an 8-hour night drive to Rome. We had the best trip ever, cracking silly jokes all the time, visiting the ancient ruins, the Vatican and museums, the Colosseum, partying in the underground clubs 'til early morning and finishing with the regular street kebab. Aww, those were the good old days!

Case Study (Travel Plans)

Traveling shall become one of your biggest life expenses. Don't let it ruin your stability. Plan, budget, be conservative, and always be on top of the best deals.

PERSONA:	Aicha M. :: 21 years old :: Egyptian Exchange city: Montreal, Canada for the fall semester Study: Foreign Politics
PROBLEM:	It's her first time in North America. She wants to see and do everything but she needs to study and doesn't have a lot of money.
SITUATION:	She thinks she won't come back for a long time after her exchange therefore she wants to maximize her 5 months stay in Montreal to travel to all the main destinations.

ACTION PLAN CONT:	She sets a travel budget of $800 per month to do 2 trips per month. After doing her research, she realized the cheapest and most efficient way to do this was to do a weekend trip and one day trip per month.
	
	September
	    • A 3.5 days bus trip to New York with InterStude with 60 other exchange students
	    • A Quebec City one day trip with InterStude
	October
	    • A Mont Tremblant day trip with the school to see the fall colors of the Canadian nature
	    • A 4.5 days Chicago, Toronto, Niagara Falls mega road trip with InterStude for a long weekend
	November
	    • An Ottawa one day trip with her Politics class
	    • A 4 days Washington, Philadelphia, Pittsburgh mega road trip with InterStude for Thanksgiving
	December
	    • A one day trip to Boston with InterStude
	    • A 7 days all inclusive trip to Cuba just before going home for Christmas

RESULTS:	Planning far ahead and doing the in-depth research allowed her to travel to 12 destinations through 23 days of intense travelling experiences.
WISDOM:	How much do you think will you be spending on traveling in your lifetime? I'm guessing hundreds if not thousands of dollars. The right planning and you learning from it will make all the difference between experiencing the whole planet and just the main attractions.

HOW TO START TRAVELING WITH LESS MONEY:

- ☐ Plan a trip doing only car sharing and couch surfing https://www.couchsurfing.com/.

- ☐ Try house-sitting or pet-sitting https://www.trustedhousesitters.com/.

- ☐ Find a data entrance or teach English online job https://t.vipkid.com.cn/.

- ☐ Crowdfund your trip https://www.fundmytravel.com/.

- ☐ Work as an au pair https://www.aupair.com/.

- ☐ Get a scholarship.

- ☐ Work on a cruise https://www.allcruisejobs.com/.

- ☐ Become a tour leader or trip sitter.

- ☐ Rent your room/apartment back home on Airbnb while you are away.

- ☐ Use miles card and credit card points to get cheap flights.

- ☐ Experience volunteering during travel to get free food and accommodation https://wwoofinternational.org/, https://www.workaway.info/.

- ☐ Become a social media influencer.

- ☐ Get a sponsorship.

TRAVELING TIPS TO BECOME A TRAVEL MASTER:

☐ Try all ways of travel: rent-a-car road trip with friends, bus tour organized group trips, sleeping on the train trip, all-inclusive resorts, and why not do hitchhiking.

☐ Travel solo to push yourself outside of your comfort zone, meeting many people on the road from different backgrounds.

☐ Don't just travel, allow yourself to slow down and savor all the details of your host city.

☐ Travel like a minimalist ready to pack in two minutes, less is more.

☐ Research, explore, but don't plan too much to not have high expectations.

☐ Be ready and embrace with laughter total disasters.

☐ Act like a confident local; if you look like an easy prey, you'll gather attention.

☐ Pay everything with your travel reward credit card to collect cash backs. Also most of those cards you pay annually offer travel insurance if you book your flight with that card.

☐ Book multi leg flights. Search what the layover cities of your potential flight to your destination are. Then use the Skyscanner app to book multi-city flights with 2–3 days apart giving you enough time to explore this new city.

Explore more travel hack tips on Chris Guillebeau's website. He had visited all 195 countries in the world before he was 35 years old. https://chrisguillebeau.com/travel-hacking-resources

FOLLOW THESE TRAVEL INFLUENCERS FOR INSPIRATION:

Top Travel Female Influencers

- https://www.instagram.com/theblondeabroad/
- https://www.instagram.com/mylifesatravelmovie/
- https://www.instagram.com/muradosmann/
- https://www.instagram.com/adventurouskate/
- https://www.facebook.com/LouisColeRules
- https://www.instagram.com/chrisburkard/
- https://www.instagram.com/damonandjo/

Top Travel Male Influencers

- https://www.instagram.com/jayalvarrez/
- https://www.instagram.com/sashajuliard/
- https://www.instagram.com/doyoutravel/
- https://www.instagram.com/everchanginghorizon/
- https://www.instagram.com/traveltomtom/
- https://www.instagram.com/byfieldtravel/

Top Travel Couple Influencers

- https://www.instagram.com/explorerssaurus_/
- https://www.instagram.com/mochilamonkeys/
- https://www.instagram.com/positravelty/
- https://www.instagram.com/xkflyaway/
- https://www.instagram.com/flipflopwanderers/
- https://www.instagram.com/onceuponajrny/https://www.instagram.com/mariefeandjakesnow/

TRAVEL COMMUNITIES TO BOND WITH OTHER TRAVEL ADDICTS:

Top Travel Conference

- https://traveleronstage.com/
- https://travelshows.com/shows/los-angeles/

- http://womenstravelfest.com/
- http://www.sheswanderful.com/witsummit/

Top Tour Companies
- https://interstude.com/
- https://www.theyachtweek.com/
- https://remoteyear.com/
- https://www.contiki.com/
- https://www.topdeck.travel/
- https://www.statravel.com
- https://lbwtravel.com/
- https://www.busabout.com/
- https://www.trutravels.com/
- https://www.bus2alps.com/

TRAVEL RESOURCES TO BECOME A MASTER TRAVELER:
Top Six Travel Books
- *Eat, Pray, Love by Elizabeth* Gilbert
- *Vagabonding* by Rolf Potts
- *The Happiness of Pursuit* by Chris Guillebeault
- *Into the Wild* by Jon Krakaeur
- *How to Travel the World on 50$ a Day* by Matt Kepnes
- *Travel as Transformation* by Gregory V. Diehl

Top Ten Travel Movies
- One Week
- The Way
- Eurotrip
- The Motorcycle Diaries
- L'auberge Espagnoles
- Little Miss Sunshine
- Eat Pray Love
- The Secret Life of Walter Mitty

- The Darjeeling Limited
- Up in the Air
- The Beach
- Into the Wild

TRAVEL EXPERIENCES YOU SHOULD DO BEFORE DYING:

Top Music Festivals
- Tomorrowland
- Burning Man
- Sziget
- Coachella
- Ultra Music Festival
- Electric Daisy Carnival
- Mawazine
- Donauinselfest

Top Nature Wonders
- Amazon Rainforest
- Iguazu Falls
- Grand Canyon
- The Great Barrier Reef
- Sahara
- Grand Prismatic Springs, Yellowstone
- Mt. Everest, Nepal

New Wonders of the World
- The Great Wall of China (China)
- Christ the Redeemer Statue (Rio de Janeiro)
- Machu Picchu (Peru)
- Chichen Itza (Yucatan Peninsula, Mexico)
- The Roman Colosseum (Rome)

- Taj Mahal (Agra, India)
- Petra (Jordan)

6 - THE DISCOVERY OF NEW PASSIONS
Exploration of yourself

Doing an exchange for a semester is all about boosting your social life to the 10x level. Everyone is always trying, attending, doing new activities or events. It is THE best time to try and test new potential hobbies. The possibilities are endless: learning a new language, cooking class, photography, painting, playing a new musical instrument, learning new soft skills, sports, volunteering, dancing classes and the list goes on without forgetting for us in Milan, Aperitivo tasting. As we said before, you usually just need to pass your classes as an exchange student and on top of that the teachers are very very flexible with you because they know that there might be some cultural differences.

My Story on the Topic...

The lifetime hobby I've picked was photography. I didn't know anything about it before leaving, but I knew I had to somehow document this journey the best I could so I bought a small pocket 16-megapixel camera, you know, the ones we had to buy separately from our cell phones before smartphones took over. It introduced me to the principles of photography and basic video editing since I wanted to summarize my journey in one video.

Later on, when we started InterStude, we took the decision to invest in a professional camera, and from those basics and curiosity on the subject, I eventually realized that I really liked doing landscape photos with a model. It became my art, my photography style. Today, anytime I need to escape the wild modern life I live in, I pick my camera up, search on Google a new landscape, find myself a friend and go shoot.

Tips for discovering a new passion:

☐ Try a few meetup.com free gatherings on all types of topics.

☐ Join paid community events or weekend gatherings to see if you connect deeply with a niche crowd of people. Do your research on Facebook Local app, Eventbrite, festicket.com or even try all kind of Airbnb experiences.

☐ Invest into a multidisciplinary online course platform to take courses on different topics. My best recommendations are masterclass.com which has a one-time fee of $189USD and SkillShare.com, which is $15USD per month. Or check individual courses on Udemy, Coursera, Linda.

☐ Explore a list of hobbies from a Google search or on Wikipedia.

Before and after you passed a few months of your life trying anything you could think of, you should sit down and create your ikigai, your reason to wake up. Google search the ikigai graph.

Start with identifying 5-10 answers in your personal and professional life to each of the FOUR ikigai quadrant questions below:

1. What do you LOVE (in your personal and professional life, the contrary of what you hate)?
2. What are you GOOD AT (that you might like or not like to do)?
3. What does the WORLD NEED (from your own perspective & vision of the world)?
4. What can I get PAID FOR (the skills you bring on the table to grow your organization)?
   Then with your answers above, do your quadrant of success:
5. What you LOVE plus you are good at (PASSION)?
6. What you don't LOVE plus you are good at (PAYING YOUR BILLS)?

7. What you LOVE plus are not good at yet (POTENTIAL) (learn more, not yet an expert)?
8. What you don't LOVE plus are not good at (DAILY TASKS)?

Finish this exercise with a purpose statement of one sentence. Make it clear that it is your reason to wake up and grow, serve people/world, give back, and inspire humans.

Watch this YouTube video of Jay Shetty for in-depth explanations

How to Find and Pursue Your Passion | Think Out Loud with Jay Shetty

7 - PARTY AND SEX
How to control addictions

Tuesday to Sunday, each day, there's a party at a new venue with a different theme. It starts right from your first week. You jumped on it because you wanted to meet as many people as you could. You might think it will slow down, but it wouldn't; even during the exam period, it will be calling you to go at least once. So why is partying such a big thing in exchange?

Well, it comes with the early twenties' urge to discover the other sex. This energy, your high libido, the sexual drive as a component of life, can affect your thoughts and may overshadow your decisions. This period of exchange will make you go to sleep super late, day after day, building a bad body clock that can lead you to fatigue and skipping classes. But be careful, skipping one class might lead you to a habit of skipping a second one and a third one.

I'm not too proud to say that it happened to me to a class I hated, I showed up to the class only once or twice in the whole semester. I then went to the final exam that counted for 100% of the class grade and, obviously, failed the exam. After a few negotiations with the teacher, she agreed to let me pass the class since I was a lost exchange student and my host university school needed to keep a good partnership with my home university.

Exchange students party tips:
- Smile, walk around alone in the venue and introduce yourself to everyone. You are the most interesting thing they will encounter this month, trust me.
- Yes, it's fun to get drunk at a young age; everyone does it. But try to have fun while being outgoing in a club without drinking. It will serve you a long way building the habit of self-confidence & control.
- You don't need to follow what everyone is doing. Too much partying can diminish the fun over time. Keep it to 1–2 times a week and go explore other experiences. It's the perfect time to discover yourself.

We come from sex. Our sexual energy is our life force energy. Open and strong sexual energy contributes towards our vitality, creativity, and sense of well-being. But sex or just sex drive alone can be a drug blocking you from creating meaningful relationships with the person you meet on a daily basis. It's more common for a young man, to think or assume when a beautiful girl smiles at him. "Oh she likes me. She thinks I'm hot. She wants to have sex with me." And then the little hamster in your head will be running all day long with fantasies and daydreams of the possibilities of maybes. A parallel unreal world way too many people stay stuck in.

Sex is a pretty taboo subject we should learn and talk more openly about. Young people nowadays educate themselves through the online porn industry. Unfortunately, their goal is not to educate you, but to get your attention as much as they can that you pass the most time on their platform; the longer you are there, the more ads are shown, the more money they earn. Therefore, they are using psychology tricks to keep you engaged that you release as much dopamine hits as possible. All this dopamine releases then lead you to lack of focus and energy in your daily life. There's even a very big new movement on YouTube called NOFAP where guys explain the killer disadvantages of watching porn and too much masturbation with counterpart health boost of cutting all those micro dopamine rush.

Another thing you most likely have never heard of is that a man should learn how to have orgasms without ejaculation; controlling the climax would lead you to multiple full body orgasms. It is also vital to keep your excess inside your body. The excess in your testicles will go right up to energize your brain, your pineal gland link to your third eye chakra. Males of 20 to 30 years old should ejaculate once every 4 days, from 30 to 40 years old, once every 8 days and so on. To learn more about this and the technique, watch this video. SEXUAL EXERCISES FOR MEN | Mantak Chia on London Real

I wish I knew when I was your age that the real true meaningful sex is spiritual sex. Not just having pleasure from your sacral chakra (orange) but from all your chakras all at once leading to a full body cosmic orgasm. Please explore the unbelievable world of Tantric sex preparing you to couple energy bounding while having sex.

Start by doing a polarity test to see if at your core you have a more feminine or masculine energy. Regardless of gender, we all contain both masculine and feminine energies. Your leading energy reflects your inner nature and values. Because of this, there are women who have masculine leading energy just as there are men who have feminine leading energy. Understanding your leading energy, or core energy, is necessary to align yourself.

Do the Erotic Blueprint quiz here to know your sex type and which one you are the most compatible with. https://surveyany-place.com/s/eroticblueprint

Here are all the explanations of the five different sex types:

- **Energetic** —the type that is turned on from not being touched as much and from anticipation, tease, and lots of space.
- **Sensual**—turned on by lots of touch, smell, aesthetics, beauty and closeness. They want bodies next to each other.
- **Sexual**—the type our culture often hails as the standard, and what it expects men to be as well. The Sexual is a very simple blueprint turned on by nudity, arousal, penetration, climax, and all the physical aspects of sexuality.
- **Kinky**—which is all about turn-ons that are taboo. Not necessarily *50 Shades of Grey* kinky, but always with a hint of naughtiness.
- **Shapeshifter**—wants everything that I just talked about, all the time, and they are often judged for being "way too much" at times in their lifetimes, but they are the most erotically sophisticated because they want it all, they can handle it all, and they can take it for hours.

"KNOWING YOURSELF IS THE BEGINNING OF ALL WISDOM."

~ ARISTOTLE

8 - RELATIONSHIPS
Experiencing human connections

As mentioned before, every one of the 16 MBTI personalities as two best matches for their friends and lovers. Those matches are made out of two opposite traits balancing yours. You need to know your two best matches and also the personalities, strengths and weaknesses of your parents, brother/sister, lover, and top five people you spend the most time with. Introspecting on all those results will give you the clarity you need to understand human social dynamics and interaction, but mainly it will show you how to love them as they are.

Another way to strengthen the bounds with your inner circle is to know their top two of their five love languages. This is coming from Gary Chapman's all-time top 20 bestselling book *The 5 Love Languages*. Take the quiz on *The 5 Love Languages* website to know what's yours.

1. **Words of Affirmation** - typically words of appreciation or praise—thanking someone for the different ways that they show love or praising someone for who they are, what they do, and what you appreciate about them.
2. **Acts of Service** - simple acts that help to make the other person's life easier or make things run smoother.
3. **Receiving Gifts** - almost always perceived as an act of love, but Chapman points out that people often don't realize that, for some, receiving gifts is the primary way through which they feel loved.

4. **Quality Time** - giving someone your undivided attention—putting away your phone and distractions and truly being with that person, whether that is having a conversation or going out and doing something together.

5. **Physical Touch** - comes in many forms—holding hands, massaging, snuggling, etc. For some, physical touch is a very important expression of love. Of course, physical touch should always be communicated clearly and consensually!

Last thing to maximize your relationships, especially your love relationship is that you should know exactly what you are looking for. By listing all the criteria of your ideal partner, you'll have an exact picture of what you need to work on to track this person in your life.

Here are Questions to Help You List the Criteria of Your Ideal Partner:

1. What does she/he look like?

2. How does she/he dress like?

3. What activities would you like to do with her/him?

4. Which subjects would you like to have conversation with her/him?

5. What are her/his qualities and weaknesses?

6. What are her/his passions and hobbies?

In exchange, you'll meet a lot of people and most likely, few people from the opposite sex. It's your time to try stuff and see what fits for you. Go all in, experience whatever that comes to mind.

9 - OUR FAMILY

Depending on your family tribe, bonding this dimension will vary. Most exchange students are lacking deep connection with their parents from the clash of generations over the fast-paced technology growth. The older generation can't adapt as fast to the younger generation's world they currently live in. This lack of deep understanding causes frustration and distance and pushes some of us to escape. And don't get me wrong here, at first, we think we are consciously on a mission to explore the world. Over the years, you might realize you were subconsciously escaping your siblings. Escaping for the need for more, for this need to become bigger, for this need to meet better things, etc. This craving for deeper meaning is the ego controlling your mind, directing your path, affecting your decisions or your need for love.

But with this first distance, a never-before-strong connection will be formed. Because it is with realizing what we lost that we realize how lucky we are that we have them. We realize that the grass is not greener on the other side. For the first time, your siblings are following you at every step, they are passionate about your daily life, you finally receive the attention you always dreamed of. On the first video call, you see gratitude in their eyes and how they are proud of you being an adult now exploring the universe.

They are so intrigued by the new you, by your new lifestyle, by the city that changed you, that is now imprinted in you, that they end up jumping with their eyes closed and wanting to come visit you. With your actions, you gave them the example, you gave them the courage to jump, you inspired them to be more, to live more, to worry less, to complain less. This visit will build your relationship stronger than ever, you'll experience adventures like you never did before. It will be by far one of the best memories you'll have with your siblings.

From this new relationship with them, your post-Erasmus transition back to your home life will be different. You'll care more about them and vice versa, you'll try to plan more activities with them, you'll have quality sessions with true mindfulness. And this new bond will help you cope more easily with post-Erasmus depression. It will give you someone to talk to about your host country who will understand and be truly interested because it's part of them now.

Activities you can do when your family visits:
- ☐ Give them a tour of your apartment and introduce them to your crazy roommates.

- ☐ Show them your three favorite spots in the city and your host university.

- ☐ Go on a weekend trip with them outside the city.

KEYNOTES SUMMARY OF THE CHAPTER:

- Research, plan, create bucket list to make the most of you exchange.

- Be aware of the don'ts to not sabotage your exchange.

- Go deep in discovering your host country's culture. It will become part of you; you'll have a second nationality.

- Master the art of the first time; you will have a lot during your exchange.

- Become a travel expert; from now on, it's going to be your biggest expense.

- Explore new potential passions and hobbies; it might lead you to finding your ikigai, your reason to wake up.

- Please learn about sacred sex and start experiencing it right now.

- Learn how to manage relationships, the hardest human skill but the most fulfilling.

- Cherish the connection with your family supporting you to this life-changing journey.

NEXT CHAPTER...

Next chapter, the saddest moment of your life. Are you ready? It's going to be SO hard, but you'll become more compassionate and grateful. No worries, I have the best tips for you to stay strong.

EXPERT
INTERVIEW :: **Jeff Chilton**

46 years old, born in Paris, never went to university but always been around the scholar environment from his dad teacher profession. Never did an exchange, but served thousands of them with his organization.

PERSONAL & BUSINESS BIO

How did you get started? Started from a friend leaving to Morocco and leaving me the management of a weekly Erasmus Party. My friend knew about my background on event management. I was directly interested from the multiculturalism aspect of it. Two years of doing those parties, I realized students were missing some needs. From housing to travel and from students' jobs to furniture.

One day, I brought two of my ambassadors German students visiting my family outside of Paris to feel real French spirit. They were a bit complaining about the Parisians being impolite. It's on the way, I realized instead of showing the countryside to two students, I should bring a whole bus. Like that, I started the Bus Tour Operator side of To Be an Erasmus in Paris.

Founder of To Be an Erasmus in Paris
https://www.tobeerasmusinparis.com/
Paris, France, Founded in 2009, 10 years old

Bus tours around France, parties, cultural events, marketplace bible web resource.

2500 students traveling per year, 13, 000 going to the events.

Market mainly from Spain, Germany, Italy. Now growing in other cities in France.

What is the thing you are most proud of? Never giving up and realizing a dream I had in 2009 of building a complete marketplace bible web resource for exchange students in France that allows them to get information, events, travel, find a room to live and find a job.

THE ERASMUS MARKET

His thoughts on the Erasmus market? Recently, I saw a reportage of the 30 years of Erasmus that passed on television. 30 years ago, leaving abroad was an extremely big adventure that someone could do. Today, the students are already backpacked in Asia or doing a month volunteering before studying abroad.

Professional skills that give the experience of a semester abroad? Being more easily open to go work abroad and taking a business opportunity. Being more autonomous to work and taking actions.

Advice given to survive the cultural shock? Be aware that the experience is a cycle; you cry when you arrive and you cry when going back home. Always be careful of the 'yes yes' answering from a tourist's standpoint being new into the country and wanting to try everything.

How to survive the post-Erasmus depression? After being welcomed by your host country, you should welcome exchange students in your country.

How to book your room for your semester abroad? Prepare well your accommodation plan because I saw way too many times students starting their semester sleeping in a hostel and finishing it in the most tiny overpriced apartment with three roommates because they couldn't find anything last minute. But I also strongly not advise people to book in advance with a deposit and contract without physically visiting the place.

Tell me a story of Erasmus student's story gone bad. An English student that contacted an agency to rent a room. The agency seemed to show all signs of professionalism with the right contract and photos of the apartment. She had to pay a deposit of 2000 Euro. The first day she arrived to the office address, she realized there was no agency and then went to the apartment address to realize that someone was already living there. She then realized she got scammed. Luckily, she had friends of her family that could host her while she could find another apartment.

What are your best travel tips for Erasmus? Bring three big 23kg suitcases, two full and one empty, because you are sure to leave with three full. After, find some good friends that can hold one of your suitcases because it will be too expensive to bring the three suitcases all at once.

Why do you think there are people that don't want to go on exchange? I think it's for financial reasons. But I don't understand why someone wouldn't take this life-changing opportunity.

THE ENTREPRENEURSHIP MINDSET

What is the accomplishment you are the most proud of? The last ten years of never giving up and never giving up in the future because things are never certain. Everything is fragile and they are never protected from a situation like the Paris terrorist attack for example.

Who inspires you the most as an entrepreneur? I don't have the time to look at what's going on in my industry around me. But I'm impressed by the founders of Facebook, Google, and Apple. All biography stories of entrepreneurs massively impacting the world with billions of people using their product. I like the biographic movie of the McDonald's founder, *The Founder.*

What are your 10-year goals? Number one, is to expand To Be An Erasmus in Paris around France. Number two, to find someone that will manage the operation so that I can get out of the day-to-day activities of the business.

Do you have any books you suggest to people?
The Little Prince by Antoine de Saint-Exupéry
Jonathan Livingston Seagull by Richard Bach

What people would be surprised to hear about you? That I would give up everything I have been working on and move on to something else in my life.

CONCLUSION

Happiness is...when I want.
Life is...beautiful.
A real entrepreneur is...the one that can get out of any troubles.
A good traveler is...a bag, shoes, and a pair of gloves.
A good exchange student is...sex, drug and rock 'n' roll.
Success is...when you received the admiration of others.

CHAPTER 5:

The End

SHOW LOVE AND GRATITUDE TO EVERYONE YOU'VE MEET

1 - THE FINAL EXAMS

Learning one semester in two weeks

The end starts here. From this point, everything goes downhill the roller coaster. It hits you out of nowhere realizing it's all about to end, but you don't want it to stop just yet, not now, not too soon; you are just adapting and fully enjoying this lifestyle. You'll need to deal with so many emotions while figuring out how to pass your final exams, and yes, passing these exams is the goal now.

You read, understand, and memorize all the concepts of a semester in two weeks for your five classes. You go on hibernation mode in your room to give it your all so you can focus on your studies and block the external world. But hey, distractions come up, even some wild friends are offering you to still go party on the weekend before the exams. Don't worry, I have all the best study and productivity tricks for you to master your exams. The best thing about this stressful period and you trying to figure out how to pull it off is that it will allow you to explore potential life-changing habits.

Case Study (Final Exams)

Managing the big day is all about preparation. It leads to confidence that will take you to a relaxed and joyful state of mind. All your life you'll be dealing with those big stressful days—a final exam, a big job interview, a public speaking presentation, your wedding, your childbirth, facing a fierce conversation, etc. Managing your inner being in those situations will set you apart from others.

PERSONA:	Ava V. :: 23 years old :: American Exchange city: Italy University: University of Bocconi | International Business
PROBLEM:	She was travelling and partying all semester so wasn't able to focus on her studies. She needs to find a way to pass her 5 final exams.
SITUATION:	Ava has 5 courses of 3 hours each a week which means she's a full time student. All her courses are in English. She only needs to pass them at 50%+ because the grades won't be noted on her USA bachelor results. The Italian system is giving you 100% of the grade of a course on the final exams. So she just showed up to every class while traveling and partying with other exchange students.

ACTION PLAN CONT:	After really enjoying her exchange, she blocked out 3 weeks of intense studying before her final exams. She prepared, took good notes from each course, did quick YouTube 5 minutes research after each class and gather resources from friends and family on each class topic. Her study plan: • Going to all her last classes until the exams • 3 hours a day of study in the morning as much as she can • Not going to any night out or events from Sunday to Friday, leaving her Saturday off • Studying by herself in her room blocking all external distractions
RESULTS:	It's all about consistency. She showed up at every class, took the main notes down on paper, organized each class into files with other resources of the web and she did herself a voice note for each class subject. Because of this she was able to review everything quickly and pass all her final exams.
WISDOM:	The Kaizen principle is the way to approach every new challenge in life. A little step every day will build consistency that will eventually be built into a lifestyle after 66 days. Take those tiny notes every day and classify them in folders linked to the other content you found. This way you won't have to stop your life to master your classes 2-3 weeks before your final exams.

FIRST, YOU NEED TO LEARN HOW TO MANAGE STRESS. HERE ARE A FEW TIPS:

- [ ] Avoid caffeine, alcohol, and nicotine.

- [ ] Indulge in physical activities.

- [ ] Get more sleep.

- [ ] Try relaxation techniques like meditation, yoga and breath work.

- [ ] Talk to someone to release some of the built-up tension.

- [ ] Note it in your journal to become more aware of the situation, 750 words morning pages without lifting your pen up the sheet.

- [ ] Manage your time and accept that you cannot do everything.

- [ ] Learn to say "no" to additional or unimportant requests.

- [ ] Decompress with friends or hobbies so that you can fall asleep with your mind not full of worries.

STUDY AND PRODUCTIVE TRICKS TO MASTER YOUR EXAMS:

- [ ] Manage your willpower by stopping draining activities and maximizing your knowledge intakes during your peek willpower time.

- [ ] You are a doer in the morning and a manager in the afternoon. Wake up early, block all distractions, create momentum with a good morning routine, and learn the new concepts needed for your exam. Take a lunch break, and in the afternoon review, refresh and practice old concepts. Take the night to decompress with a dinner with a friend, do some creative hobbies, take a warm bath, etc. Start again the day after. Watching a movie or series doesn't make you decompress.

Always "Eat The Frog". Your most demanding tasks, tasks you usually try to avoid, should be the first thing you do. The tasks you hate the most.

☐ The only way to really learn something is by taking action. Don't expect to understand the content by just reading while underlining and then rereading 2–3 times and taking notes. That's the robot technique they teach you at school. Explore YouTube videos on the topic, find and call an expert on LinkedIn, Clarity.fm, Table.com, etc. to get their insight, first-hand experience on the topic.

☐ Go visit a local company asking them to talk to the person in Human Resource and tell them that you are highly inter-ested in their company culture, and from there, you sneak your way into asking questions that might lead you to a better prospect or directly to the information you are curious about. If you create a strong connection, they could even give you an opportunity to volunteer for a day or a week get-ting a mini internship. Be bold, pushy, excited, curious, and a deep listener.

Make sure to understand the content of your textbooks, but don't focus on them. The university textbook industry is a scam; they are trying to produce big volumes of books filled with defi-nitions so that they can sell it to you at a bigger price. You are paying $200–300 for a textbook when you could learn way more in-depth and faster by doing your own research.

Here's how to manage your willpower. Willpower is like your cell phone battery, it starts the day fully charged at 100% and drains itself slowly overtime. But there are things that drain your willpower way faster just like those heavy apps that drain your phone battery.

Here's the list of things that drain your willpower more quickly:
- Stress
- Implementing new behavior (example a new workout habit)
- Filtering distraction (notifications, TV, phone, people)
- Resisting temptation
- Suppressing emotions
- Restraining aggressions
- Suppressing impulses
- Taking tests
- Trying to impress others
- Coping with fear
- Doing something you don't like to do
- Selecting long-term over short-term results, etc. (separate your big projects in smaller day goals)
- Negative thoughts

You can only fully recharge your willpower with a good eight hours of sleep finishing five deep Rapid Eye Movement (REM) sleep cycle. But you can slightly recharge it with a ten-minute meditation, a 20-minute sunbath, a 12-minute power nap, and eating colorful organic fruits and vegetables, barefoot earth grounding, sacred sex, and small 20-minute workouts.

Here's a morning routine example to create momentum to pull your best morning studies/work. Start small, pick up 3–4 things in it, list it into a schedule like this below and print it to start focusing on your new morning routine.

7h30: "Wake up with Determination Alarm" motivation soundtrack

7h30–7h45:
1. Remove earplugs, fold the pillow in two to lift my head, get up to shut down the alarm, thoughts monitoring (10 min)
2. Go pee, smile in the mirror, turn on a happy vibe music, drink cold water, brush your teeth with your reverse hand
3. 1-minute workout yoga stretching

7h45–8h20:
4. Make my bed and 5-minute journal affirmation, positive statement, love, gratitude and one goal setting
5. 10 minutes body weight or jump rope workout

8h20–8h50:
6. Cold Shower
7. Get dressed, do my hair, cream, perfume, etc., get ready to go out
8. Drink cold-pressed green juice and eat fruits
9. Review 3-year vision, tasks and goals of the day and week

Not-to-do list:
1. Don't have big breakfast or coffee before your 'one' thing
2. Don't leave the house without a first 1h30 work on your 'one' thing
3. Don't open communication apps and any spirits infiltrer

You may find interesting the advice to take a cold shower in the morning. Studies have shown that cold shower has so many benefits that you can't just disregard.

Here are the benefits of a cold shower:
- **Increases Alertness.** The deep breathing in response to our body's shock helps us keep warm, as it increases our overall oxygen intake. Thus, our heart rate will also increase, releasing a rush of blood through our entire body. This gives us a natural dose of energy for the day.
- **Refines Hair and Skin.** Hot water has a tendency to dry out our skin, so it's best to use cold water to tighten your cuticles and pores, preventing them from getting clogged.
- **Improves Immunity and Blood Circulation.** Cold water can improve circulation by encouraging blood to surround our organs, which can then help combat some problems of the skin and heart
- **Stimulates Weight Loss.** Cold showers can promote brown fat activity. Brown fat is the good fat which generates heat to keep our bodies warm and is activated when exposed to extreme cold.
- **Speeds Up Muscle Soreness and Recovery.** We have all seen athletes taking ice baths after training to reduce muscle soreness, but a quick cold shower after breaking a sweat at the gym can be just as effective, especially in relieving delayed-onset muscle soreness.
- **Eases Stress.** Jumping into the shower without letting it heat up, or going into the ocean without slowly acclimating to it, can help promote resilience, increasing tolerance to stress and even disease.
- **Relieves Depression.** Cold showers have been shown to relieve depression symptoms due to the intense impact of cold receptors in the skin which send an overwhelming

amount of electrical impulses from the peripheral nerve endings to the brain.

- **Boosts fertility.** Another interesting benefit of cold showers is that they will boost your sperm count and increase fertility.
- **Builds strong will power.** Doing something you are so resistant to, every single day, *right when you wake up*, takes a lot of mental strength. And overtime, this mental strength and discipline will become an automated habit that echoes into every area of your life.

The cold shower got popularized massively through Wim Hof, the Iceman who constantly defeated world records and is now encouraging normal people to do the same to heal their diseases and depression with the cold. Watch this VICE documentary: Inside the Superhuman World of the Iceman

Here's a night routine example to maximize your REM sleep so you wake up in full strength for your morning routine.

23h00: "Evening Routine Alarm" ringtone

23h00–23h40:
1. A hot shower and drink cold water after
2. Brush my teeth

23h40–00h00:
3. Journaling five minutes about a positive thing that happened today

Not-to-do list:
1. Don't eat and check your phone after 20h30
2. Don't plan & set goals for tomorrow after 18h00
3. Don't eat heavy food or dairy for dinner

Here's an ideal day example to satisfy your Seven Wellness Life Dimension (Appendix) and go to sleep with deep satisfaction and wake up with excitement to relive the same day.

7h30–9h00: Morning Routine

9h00–10h30: Work at Home on My One Thing (Maker)

10h30–11h00: Breakfast break

11h00–12h30: Work at Home on My One Thing (Maker)

12h30–13h00: Walk, Relax, Read

13h00–14h00: Management, Communication (Manager)

14h00–14h30: Lunch Break

14h30–15h00: Meditation and Planning Tomorrow

15h00–19h00: Passion, Learning, Exploring

19h00–20h30: Dinner with Friends

20h30–23h00: Relationship Activities

23h00–00h00: Night Routine

00h00–7h30: Sleep 7h30 minimum

Exchange Student's Story...

There are always some stories gossiped around the Erasmus community. One of the stories I've heard was about a guy who challenged himself and announced to his friend that he would travel all the semester with his scholarship money and only show up to do all the final exams while managing to pass them all.

Yes, I know what you are thinking - What the hell, that's not fair! I've even heard of another story of two friends who came back to Canada during their second semester of one-year exchange and accordingly they worked, made money while skipping all classes, and took a flight back to do their final exams. Unfortunately, all these are possible because some teachers give you a kind of a free pass since they don't want to hurt the Erasmus program and universities' partnership reputation.

While we are here talking about maximizing your life and productivity, here's a tip towards your Ideal Year—a yearly routine of vacations and world-class lifestyle habits.

Ideal Year

{Objective: Work between vacations, don't work for a vacation. You are paid to rest, learn, think and delegate, not to work. A clear mind empty of worries and full of joy is the key to productivity}

January–February
- New city, new culture, new friends. Enjoy an active social life
- Two months of gathering and classifying your studies knowledge

March–April
- Ten days off for Spring Break, go explore something instead of drinking like animals
- One month of hard study
- May–June–July
- Summer internship abroad
- Ten days' spiritual retreat

August
- Preparation and Planning of the school year

September–October
- New school year. Enjoy an active social life
- Two months of gathering and classifying your studies knowledge
- Ten days' discovery trip

November–December
- 1.5 months to study hard and finish your personal goals of the year
- 14 days Christmas holiday family trip

2 - THE DEPARTURE OF A FEW
They fall like dominoes

When you hear that the first person in your exchange is leaving, it hits you by surprise and you start asking yourself questions; slowly, you start thinking about the old life waiting for you. You feel the need to start planning your future, how you'll overcome post-Erasmus depression, how you'll gather back with your home friends. The problem with all these is that your mind is no longer in your exchange abroad; you are not being fully present to enjoy the last few weeks.

My story on the topic...

I planned my shot ahead. I knew I didn't want to come back right away to Montreal after my exchange and I wanted to enjoy the summer in Europe, so I booked a roundway flight that was coming back early September, the day that my classes restarted in Canada.

As fellow exchange students started to leave, I wondered how I was going to spend my summer. I started to ask suggestions from other exchange students and also inquired about their own summer plans until I ended up in a dinner where one of my friends randomly exclaimed, "You should go pass the summer in the Greek Islands!" and at the same time everyone got excited. So that's what I did. I booked a flight to Athens and thought I would figure it all out upon my arrival and by meeting people at the hostel.

3 - THE LAST PARTY
Joy, sadness, loneliness, extravagance, frustration

There are all kinds of last party experiences, but the thing they all have in common is that they will make you nostalgic because it's an official end event reunion. If you are lucky enough to have a dedicated exchange students organization like MIEO Colombia, you will experience an official exchange students goodbye party with a traditional honored ceremony of giving certificates to the king/queen of the semester, the party master, the cutest, etc. where everyone makes his fellow exchange sign his host country flag or special souvenir like a t-shirt or a notebook. This kind of dedicated detail makes it even more memorable. The last party will be bizarre, you'll have fun, but you're sad on the inside.

My Story on the Topic...

My roommate, Imran, and I had a big balcony at the student residence we stayed at. Though I only stayed at that student residence for a month, I kept a strong friendship with Imran throughout the semester. We ended up having the brilliant idea to invite everyone we knew to do a beer pong and BBQ party at the balcony. It was memorable; I'm still nostalgic when I look at our photos.

Erasmus Goodbye party tips:

☐ Hug everyone you love as hard as you can on the right side, heart-to-heart connection.

☐ Make all your fellow exchange students sign your souvenir flag from your host country.

☐ Get drunk but not dead drunk one last time doing silly stuff.

☐ Video testimonials of your best friends about the journey you've been together.

4 - GOODBYE, ROOMMATES
A new family

It's not only the goodbye party that makes it official, but also the last roommates' dinner. Most likely, you will be part of the organization of this big feast. The whole process of scheduling, planning, buying, preparing and enjoying this dinner night will make you very nostalgic. Everyone will do his best to make it as perfect as possible, but when the time to actually eat arrives, there you'll feel that you are not even hungry from all the mental energy you put on the organization. You let your roommates enjoy and you observe them with love.

Slowly over the dinner, the wine starts to go down and the atmosphere will shift over stories of the semester and gossips of one of your roommates unveiled. At that point, the laughters are thrown everywhere. These people have become your second family in a very short period of time. You'll forever think of them and will hope to hug them again even after years apart. As you part ways, initially, you'll reach out to them and give them the news about your new life. You'll send them some gifts and photos. And one day, maybe, you'll see them all again at the same time, have a big family dinner that will freeze time.

Goodbye, roommates tips:
- ☐ Prepare a massive dinner night with a lot of wine.

- ☐ Give each other gifts from your country they can cherish all their life.

- ☐ Make them sign your host country flag (or t-shirt or notebook).

- ☐ Take a last group picture at the dinner table.

5 - HOLIDAYS BEFORE GOING HOME
The transition needed

One of the best tips to have a less crushing post-Erasmus depression is to have a long trip after your exchange and before going back home.

My story on the topic...

As mentioned earlier, I decided to spend the summer alone in the Greek Islands without really knowing what I was getting into. For me, it's all about the beauty of traveling - freestyle, no planning, jumping into the unknown, but I understand there's a type of traveler per MBTI personality.

The trip started really well while discovering the ancient ruins of Athens while being shocked with the downtown mess and dirt, but at the same time falling in love with the local food. I had one of the best meals of my life in a small pedestrian touristy street of Athens. It was my first ever Moussaka, never heard of this dish before, but from the first bite I fell in love with the whole country, the universe and its humanity. All the perfect simple mix of those flavors was a real mouth orgasm.

I then headed quickly to the ferry to start my island hopping. Obviously, I started with the most famous beauty, Santorini. How incredible is the scenery matched with its atmosphere of peace, you would like to just live and die on this island. After going on a day trip boat exploration, I headed to my main destination, Ios. Ios is the underground party island full of solo bar owners. I've heard I could hang out in Ios for a very cheap price while living in a camping ground while working at a bar under the table. And so I did.

After 1–2 weeks, I finally found a front door salesperson job at a bar working every night at getting people in the bar and every afternoon cleaning the bar. It was one of the worst working experiences I had in my life. The boss was treating workers like shit and even threatening they would be in trouble if they didn't show up to the job. Back then, I thought he was just the worst human being on the entire planet, but from what I know of human psychology now, he was just extremely sad and lonely inside, beaten up by the society's game and not having fixed his trapped emotions. This guy was scaring me so much that I was so afraid to quit the job until after weeks of bad party lifestyle I caught sinusitis.

Stuck in bed and unable to move, they had to send me back to Athens since there was no proper hospital on the island. After painfully making it to the hospital and surviving the wait of the general emergency procedures and paperwork, they prescribed antibiotics. I was ten days in bed drinking water and eating soft food. I had enough of this summer journey in Greece, the only thing I wanted now is to go back home. I tried to change my return flight to Canada, but that was just too expensive, I had no more money, I was surviving in the cheapest hostel in town while eating 2€ Gyros every meal. The only solution I've found with my situation was to talk with my old roommates in Milan and convinced them to let me stay for free for one month while I was waiting for my flight back home.

Summer time in Milan is not the best, everyone is gone in the south or on the coast; the city is empty. With no money, I decided to start my self-development journey from learning everything I put my hand on about the mysterious world of Pick-up Artist. I basically didn't go out much out my room for a month amazed with this content going down the rabbit whole of infinite social dynamics knowledge. But what I didn't know back then is that knowledge is not power, action and practice on that knowledge is, leading to in-depth experience.

Post-Erasmus long trip options:
- https://www.workaway.info/
- https://wwoofinternational.org/
- https://www.goatsontheroad.com/
  things-to-do-in-ios-greek-island/
- https://www.nomadtrain.co/
- https://www.nomadcruise.com/
- https://www.topdeck.travel/
- https://www.volunteerhq.org
- https://www.gooverseas.com/
- https://www.idealist.org

Post-Erasmus long trip tips:

☐ It should be a minimum 3–4 weeks trip.

☐ Try to go with friends that were not from your Erasmus; post-Erasmus depression transition will be easier.

☐ Do something super unique, go on the unbeaten path, try something you'll never do again in your life. Hitchhiking, mega road trip crossing 3000+km, volunteering work, a long sea trip, etc.

KEYNOTES SUMMARY OF THE CHAPTER:

- Learn how to master productivity and knowledge.

- Be mentally prepared for the start of the departures of a few.

- Make the most of the last party; it will be a lifetime memories.

- Pass quality time one last time with your roommates, your second family.

- Don't go home right away after your exchange; jump on a last big trip. It will help the transition.

NEXT CHAPTER...

Next chapter, living with a massive upgrade of yourself in a home town you don't recognize. Are you ready? It's going to be challenging, but from suffering comes wisdom. No worries, I have the best tips to give you all the mental support you'll need.

The *Depression*

IT'S GOING TO BE SO HARD TO MOVE ON

1 - THE RETURN FLIGHT
Insomnia and all kinds of thoughts

What was that all about? Looking back and remembering this life experience, you'll constantly have this mixed emotions, you'll feel the need to cry, it'll be a mix of nostalgia and sadness that will slightly squeeze your heart. You'll experience this feeling initially during your return flight and this will never go away all your life. But whenever these thoughts come to mind, counter them with positive affirmations, acknowledge this as a celebration of life, how you played the game, how this experience has given you a new standard and a constant reminder to live your life to the fullest.

The flight home is the toughest part of the journey. You'll cry in the plane, that's certain. It's official now, it's all over. You'll be dreaming to go back, to relive those experiences, to have this strong community lifestyle, to travel and explore as much as you did. You'll have the impression that your heart remained somewhere else. But there's also a funny part to this end, most exchange students arrive at their destination with one 23kg luggage, but leave with two 23kg luggage as mentioned in the Jeff Chilton interview.

Another weird moment will be your transport experience from the airport to your family home. You'll be shocked how you are now analyzing your home city from another angle. Arriving home, realizing nothing has changed, you don't want to touch anything as you're too scared to go back to your old life routine.

Return flight tips:
- ☐ Cycle back your journal entry with an end-of-the-experience analysis.

- ☐ Classify your photos or start a video edit of photos from your best moments.

- ☐ Meet someone on the plane to create a connection with your host country and your home country. Maybe you could meet again this person for a coffee in your first week home.

2 - POST-EXCHANGE DEPRESSION
Everything is boring

Depression, the planet's biggest epidemic, but this is not a disease like the pharmaceutical are trying to sell you; it is a state of mind where all your conscious attention is center to yourself, your own little existence. When you stop thinking of your life's situation and you start thinking of how you can help, give, love others while starting your spiritual journey with meditation and yoga combined with readings like *The Power of Now* or *The Untethered Soul*, you start taking control of your mind. You can either control your mind or it will control you, this millions of years old machine that is there to keep you alive and protect you at any means.

As Jeff Chilton mentioned, "The exchange students' experience makes you cry two times: once you arrive and once you leave." To go even more in-depth, the student exchange experience destroys the old you. Your adaptation back to the normal life will most likely make you insane. Everyone doesn't understand what you've been through. You lack true connection with people who don't excite you. You try to adapt, but you can't figure it out. You can't find comfort with the norm. You bury yourself into travel movies or life-changing international experience documentaries, anything you can find to inspire you to something more.

Post-Erasmus Depression tips:
- ☐ Join an initiative or help out on welcoming exchange students in your hometown.

- ☐ Plan a calendar of weekly social activities to make sure you don't stay in your room thinking about the past.

- ☐ Plan another big life-changing experience like an internship abroad, a second exchange, a volunteering travel experience, or an international business case.

Planning on another life-changing experience will bring you the energy boost you need to change your thoughts. While waiting for your next studies abroad, internship abroad, or work travel permit, do one of these life-changing travel experiences:
- Go on Safari in Tanzania,
- Heli-skiing in Girdwood, Alaska
- Drink beer at Oktoberfest in Munich
- Throw tomatoes at La Tomatina in Spain
- Find your mojo at a yoga retreat in Pune, India

- Take a pastry cooking class in France
- Meet the Moai at Easter Island
- Marvel the Northern Lights in Sweden
- Try new wine at Beaujolais days in France
- Try on a mask at Venice carnival
- Dive at the Great Barrier Reef
- Visit Hobbiton in New Zealand
- See sunrise over Bagan Temples in Myanmar
- Climb Iconic Sydney Harbour Bridge
- Bungee Jump at Bhote Koshi River, near Kathmandu
- Ride the Glacier Express in Switzerland
- Watch Komodo dragons in Indonesia
- Hike Taman Negara National Park, Malaysia
- Take a boat ride down the Ganges at Varanasi
- Spend a night at a deserted island
- Swim at the infinity pool at Marina Bay Sands in Singapore
- Watch the sunrise and sunset at Uluru, Australia
- Climb Table Mountain, Cape Town, South Africa
- Admire Yellowstone National Park, Wyoming, USA
- Swim at the Blue Lagoon in Island
- Watch whales in the Gulf of St Lawrence, Canada
- Observe mysterious Nazca lines in Peru
- Explore the world's driest place: the Atacama Desert in Chile
- Take a slow ride up the Mekong in Laos
- Learn to dance salsa in Havana, Cuba
- Husky mush in Lapland, Sweden
- Temple-gaze at Abu Simbel, Egypt
- Climb Kilimanjaro in Tanzania
- Go trekking around Annapurna circuit in Nepal
- Visit Baliem Valley in Papua, Indonesia
- Walk along the Great Wall of China
- Sneak to Tiger's Nest in Bhutan

- Try on a maiko or geiko outfit in Kyoto
- Japan, Marvel the palaces in Lhasa, Tibet
- Ride the Trans-Siberian Railway across Russia
- Cross the Salar de Uyuni salt flats in Bolivia
- Snorkel with manta rays in Bora Bora, French Polynesia
- Meet mountain gorillas in Rwanda
- Get carried away at Machu Picchu in Peru
- Visit a tea ceremony in Japan
- Catch the sunrise at the Taj Mahal in Agra
- Admire Michelangelo paintings at Sistine Chapel, Vatican
- Treat yourself with spa at Bodrum, Turkey
- Meet sunrise over Angkor Wat in Cambodia
- Step closer to the edge at the rock city of Sigiriya, Sri Lanka[1]

3 - YOU ARE AN AMBASSADOR
Talk about your experience to everyone

The best marketing in the world is the word-of-mouth because people are more inclined to trust a friend than online reviews or public relations articles. In having a friend's direct recommendation, you have already started to build a personal connection with the brand/service. If your exchange really made you the person you are today, it is therefore your duty to spread the word and let the most number of people experience the same.

After your exchange, you become part of the millions of ambassador of the exchange students' experience. You can bond with this

---

[1] https://www.lifehack.org/articles/lifestyle/50-incredible-travel-experiences-have-once-your-life.html

worldwide community via online group and even attend alumni events. But the best way you'll ever give back is to spread the word to people.

Erasmus exchange ambassador tips to spread the word-of-mouth:

- ☐ Write a blog post about your whole experience or a specific topic of exchange.

- ☐ Post on social media a video summary of your experience.

- ☐ Present your experience in your home university classes while telling people why they should leave.

- ☐ Write a testimonial of your experience to be used by your university international students desk.

- ☐ Help your university international students desk during their several events promoting this opportunity.

- ☐ Volunteer one semester for the students association or organization that satisfy the social life of exchange students in your city or university.

4 - A NEW YOU
Your little magic souvenir box

First, there's the place where you are born and where you grow up. Then there's the place that adopts you for a semester, the time you build yourself. And finally, there are also the nations that we adopt by connecting with so many international friends, we live in multicultural diverse situations so enriching they transform us.

Our home remains our home, but all of a sudden, we feel like a citizen of the world, we are part of the global citizen nation. You don't look at people the same way in the subway. You no longer see the architecture of your city buildings the same way. Even the news you read does not affect you the same way. When there's a crisis in Turkey, you worry about your Turkish exchange friends; when the world cup is won by France, you immediately get a view from the inside of the country's celebration; or when there's a historical political moment happening in the United States, you become part of the debate with your American friends.

From all these memories and connections, you need to create for yourself a magical fortress of souvenirs. At first, it might be a full redecoration of your room with a photo wall of fame, hanging your host country flag signed by dozens of exchange friends and placing all your physical souvenirs on your library shelf. But after a while, you'll have to stop looking at those souvenirs to really move on to the next stage of your life and get out of the post-Erasmus depression. Create yourself a beautiful magical souvenir box where you classify all your exchange souvenirs and over the years go through them to bring back the gratitude of those moments.

5 - KEEPING CONTACT WITH OUR EXCHANGE FRIENDS
They will be never forgotten

Keeping contact with most exchange students friends will be impossible, and even as a group, the community will dissolve rapidly over 3–4 months after the exchange. You might reach out some-day to some exchange that you thought you would connect just like the good old days, but when asking them how their lives have been, they might respond with the lines, 'I don't know, it's been so long since we didn't talk'. In the end, you'll realize there wasn't much to say, everyone came back to real life, studying, working.

But there will be a few true international friends that no matter how long you stayed apart, once you see them again, it will feel just like yesterday and you'll reconnect exactly where you left off like distance and time didn't exist. Their new jobs didn't boost their ego, they didn't get assimilated by the system, they stayed true to their inner child and funky self doing crazy things just like what they've been doing during the exchange.

But don't forget you are now part of the Erasmus Family; there are thousands of friends you haven't met yet. Here's a list of values that connect us all:

- Global Citizen mindset
- Exploring the world
- Freedom
- Equality
- Creativity and expression
- Courage
- Peace, love, compassion, understanding, and gratitude
- Fun
- Positive attitude
- Quality time together
- Volunteer work
- Being open-minded to new things
- Encouraging each family member to pursue their dreams

The ultimate tip on that topic is that you need to organize a weekend trip reunion one year after your exchange in one central city in the world gathering as much exchange friends as possible. A weekend back in time to show gratitude for each other and celebrate life one last time together. This will be a unique experience that will touch your heart.

6 - YOUR PROFESSIONAL LIFE AFTER ERASMUS
Skills surpassing others

Backed by his ten years of entrepreneurship experience, Jeff Chilton stood by the difference when it comes to productivity and micro management; there's a huge difference between a person who lived, studied, or worked abroad versus someone who didn't. The difference is so big that he now makes sure to hire only people who lived abroad. As mentioned before, take note of your MBTI personality traits before leaving and evaluate them after your exchange to see how you have changed.

Here's the list of top skills that your experience abroad gave you. Put them upfront during interviews to promote yourself:
- Independence
- Creative problem solving
- Patience
- Multidisciplinary thinking
- Ambition
- Meeting new people, making new friends, being outgoing
- International experience knowing the world
- Cultural understanding
- Multicultural engagement
- Self-management
- Self-confidence
- Maturity
- Initiative, taking actions
- Being spontaneous
- Resilience
- Global connections

Case Study *(Career Post Erasmus)*

PERSONA:	Marie F. :: 22 years old :: French Exchange city: Sydney, Australia University: University of Sydney
PROBLEM:	Marie has just returned home from her exchange to finish her last bachelor degree semester. She hopes to find a job she can be passionate with after graduation.
SITUATION:	Her purpose: "My reason to wake up is to use my creative audiovisual skills to inspire and help more bachelor degree French students through educational videos, to go on an abroad experience in English to fully face the globalization market we live in." Therefore, she decided to apply as a Marketing Coordinator at travel and abroad experiences organizations to get some experience in the field. After long hours of web research on job websites and asking around on Facebook groups, she listed down her top 5 options where she would be delighted to work for. Here's her top 5: Top Deck Tours Remote Year Erasmus Students Network Culture Trip Selina Hostel HQ She's so excited about working for these organizations that she made sure to create a very detailed and personal cover letter for each of them. She sent her Linkedin profile to the recruitment emails she found. She then found the recruitment managers on Linkedin whom she messaged personally on top of trying to find people, employee references inside the organization.

RESULTS:	Her passion and enthusiasm got the attention of Top Deck Tours and Remote Year. She went through the full 3-steps recruitment process for both companies and both offered her a position aligned with her desires in terms of conditions and responsibilities.
WISDOM:	When you really put yourself out there doing the right research and applying with all your heart to a job you are extremely excited about, it makes all the difference. And for sure like any sales deal you need to push, reach out in all ways possible, and learn by heart the background of the business and the recruitment manager who will be interviewing you. The employers surely recognize those little details and your excitement giving you the edge above everyone else. I myself only hire extremely excited driven people who wanted so much to work for me or my company that they would do it for free.

TIPS FOR FINDING A JOB SATISFYING YOUR GLOBAL CITIZEN MINDSET:

☐ Before starting, list down all your skills and resources, including the ones you got abroad. Skills, experiences, contacts, physical goods, knowledge, etc., everything you can leverage during a job interview.

☐ Don't look for a job that interests you, look for an industry first. Most of you would love the travel industry, social enterprise industry, volunteering industry, startup industry.

☐ A strong company culture is more important than the right job. You need to find a company that has a cultural link to your values mentioned before. Multiculturalism, remote work, intrapreneurship, self-growth, team building, love, openness, etc.

☐ The first boss you'll have when starting your career will highly influence your entire career by the foundation and habits he will pass onto you. Make sure to have a strong connection with this person and that you genuinely feel he's an inspiring person.

☐ In your cover letter for applying for a job, make sure to talk about your study abroad experience with all the skills it has given you and why not talk about a nice travel peripeti you have learned from. Also, it's obvious, but make sure to customize your cover letter uniquely for the company you are applying for while linking your values with their values and current projects from your online research on them.

☐ Why not try to start your career in the exchange students / study abroad industry, you are an expert now.

Good job offer websites:
- https://co.indeed.com/
- https://www.glassdoor.com/
- https://remote.com/
- https://remoteok.io/
- https://workew.com/
- https://www.linkedin.com/jobs/
- Jobs near me Google search

The Erasmus Program is also a surprising program to explore for entrepreneurs. Give it a look if you are from Europe. There's also an incubator for Erasmus Alumni called ESAA. Finally, there's a marketplace where Erasmus Alumni help each other with their professional skills called Garage Erasmus.

7 - VISITING YOUR ERASMUS CITY AGAIN IN THE FUTURE
The meeting with your old extravagant self

There's nothing like visiting your Erasmus city years later. But there are some people who miss Erasmus so much that they go back to their host cities not too long, after a year or so post exchange. The problem with this is that you end up being disappointed of not having the same kind of lifestyle from your Erasmus days. Somehow, you'll feel that the city is a bit more boring without this strong community. The best is to really wait 3+ years when you have already overcome the post-Erasmus depression and moved on with a new lifestyle. Then you'll experience the city from a whole new perspective, still full of nostalgia.

If you have the chance to visit it with a good friend or a family member, it's even better because you'll be walking around like a tour guide giving all your thoughts and insights about each place close to your heart. You'll even be the best tour guide ever from engaging with so much passion with all the feelings all those places gave you.

Here's a list of places to visit and things to do when you go back to your host city:

☐ The heart center of the city where everyone passes by.

☐ The best landscape view of the city.

☐ Take a long metro or public transport ride observing people on their daily life.

☐ Your host university campus and why not meet an old teacher.

☐ Your favorite restaurant.

☐ Your favorite bar or club.

☐ Your favorite street food.

☐ Your ex-apartment or student residence.

☐ Go have a coffee with your top local friends.

☐ Go take a before & after photo exactly at the same spot you did in the past with the same angle and gesture and why not similar clothes.

My Story on the Topic...

I always dreamed of going back to the city that changed me. From an exchange friend's Facebook post, I saw a lot of people did go back in the first two years after our life-changing adventure. I paid high attention to their story going back and I was jealous. I was planning to pass by Milan five years after while I was back in Europe for the summer, but I had to cut my trip short and go back home.

Unexpectedly, six years after my exchange, the universe placed all the dots giving me a crazy opportunity I jumped on. I randomly jumped on a plan to visit my Italian new girlfriend I met in Montreal who was about to start a new job in Milan. I jumped with all my heart on a plan to surprise her at the exit of her job. It was a 15-hour flight. It was freezing. I wasn't wearing a coat. I waited for three hours outside with my backpack trying to pull the best surprise ever. And it was magical.

We ended up living in Milan together for a little while discovering again this charming city. I was able to revisit all my exchange students' spots. This period in time was just priceless.

KEYNOTES SUMMARY OF THE CHAPTER:

- Use the return flight to close the loop of the experience and introspect on it in your journal.

- Depression is a state of mind that you can shift. Use the many tricks to control your mind or it will control you.

- You are an expert, teacher, mentor now. Go be the light that you wish you would have had before leaving on exchange.

- Follow on your exchange students community remembering the incredible time together.

- There's the perfect job for you out there. Ask the universe, believe it and manifest it with deep research, enthusiastic application and never giving up till you get the interview.

- Go back visiting your host exchange city with a brand new perspective.

Conclusion

"WHEN OVERSEAS YOU LEARN MORE
ABOUT YOUR OWN COUNTRY,
THAN YOU DO THE PLACE YOU'RE VISITING."

~ CLINT BORGEN

Abroad, students see so many things, their eyes sparkle contin-
uously. They meet so many people, travel to so many places, and
discover so many things. They also share a lot. It's so amusing to be
able to cook a Poutine for Italians, whereas here, this dish seems
banal to us. It's so great to be able to exchange musical knowledge and sell our Montreal artists while discovering Colombian
music type you never heard about before. It's so fascinating to talk
about Quebec identity with English Canadians, talk politics with
Americans, and talk about the economic crisis with Greeks. When
one opens up to the rest of the world, the hours pass like seconds.
Everything is going so fast, or maybe the time just stop.

We fall in love with a unique way to live like an innocent child
discovering every little thing in life for the first time. But when we
go home, we lose everything, even this innocent curious mind. But
with suffering comes wisdom and it's in that moment of darkness
that you'll understand the truth - the real way of living this journey is to be fully mindful at every moment in every conversation

we have, every project we create, every support we give, every sex movement we do, every bite we eat, every feet we put forward, every breath we take, every hug we give, every word we praise.

In this, we'll realize that the life that has been sold to us is a trap, a rat race sold by Hollywood, the corporations' shareholders and the avid marketers trying to get our attention. We don't need a lot of money, we don't need to buy stuff, we don't need to become bigger than ourselves, we don't need to get the recognition of people we don't know, we don't need to find a partner who will complete us. All we need is to experience life no matter where we are in this world with full presence connecting with fellow humans with love, peace, understanding, compassion, praise, hugging from the right side for a heart-to-heart connection and around a community lifestyle where we support and love each other for the way we all are.

You will connect your whole life with people who would have lived an exchange. Those nostalgic conversations will hit you right to your core. It will carry you all your life. Please help us bring the awareness of this life-changing opportunity. Let's boost the word-of-mouth.

Thank you so much for reading this book, it means everything to me. I've put all my love and experiences here to hopefully make an impact. I started this book five years ago and stopped. Then, one day, I've found the courage to finish it over a six-month period. This is my legacy to the Erasmus exchange student market. Hope you can share it to your friends and family that they understand what you lived and what you have become. Please don't forget to write an Amazon review, as your support means everything.

Jf Brou
Xoxo

If you need anything, don't hesitate. I'm here for you. But remember, all the answers are inside you. Meditate.

Appendix 1

EIGHT STEPS TO UNFUCK YOURSELF FROM YOUR CONDITIONING TO BECOME YOUR BEST VERSION

Escape your parents and environment patterns

Society builds us all into unwanted patterns that stop us from blooming into the masterpiece we could become. It is our own job to dig deep, find our own answers of our conditionings, and work on separating ourselves from it.

1 - KNOW YOUR MBTI PERSONALITY TRAITS, OF YOUR PARENTS, AND OF YOUR TWO BEST MATCHES

The most common personality test used worldwide. Helps you learn about your strengths & weaknesses, romantic relationships, friendship, parenthood, career path, workplace habits and more. Make the test here in 12 minutes.

Then identify your two best relationships match for best friends, business partners and spouse. In blue on the relationship chart.

For the best of you guys, take the Hexaco test to know if you are a good asset in your organization with your level of Agreeableness and Conscientiousness.

And for the craziest of you, make the Dark Triad, known as the antisocial test. Every entrepreneur, actor, model, stripper, etc. start their journey with very high Machiavellianism and high Narcissism.

2 - GO DEEP WITH INTROSPECTION EXERCISES TO KNOW YOURSELF BETTER THAN FACEBOOK DOES

* Analyse everyone you had a physical or virtual conversation with in the last month. List their names and grade them on 1 to 10 without using the number 7 (safe, good, ok spot). You evaluate them on how you felt after the conversation: more energy, happy, enthusiastic, etc. or drained, stressed, demotivated, etc.
* List all your bad habits that are making you lose time, energy, money, relationships. We are creatures of habit, when you start micro-analysing. it you'll realize habits everywhere: List all GOOD habits you are proud of that give you an edge on other people.
* Ask 10–20 of your current and past colleagues, "Hey, I'm doing an introspection exercise. What do you think is my strongest professional skill? You should improve that skill to become an expert at it. When you work one hour with that skill, you provide the most return to your business or organization.
* List your top ten values you live with or would like to live by and then circle your top three behaviors that make you act on those values daily/weekly even if you are exhausted or have no time that day/week.

- What are all the emotions you lived in the last week, what happened and why? (negative emotions are patterns that need to be broken).
- List your resources (knowledge, contacts, skills, colleagues, assets, experiences, material, etc.).
- What do you like and don't like to do? (Personal & Professional life).

3 - ANALYSE YOUR CHILDHOOD, YOUR PAST, YOUR LIFE NOW AND PROJECT IN THE FUTURE

PAST

- What was the best day of your life and Why?
- LOVE begins at home. Who in the family has been in the past unwanted, unloved, uncared, forgotten?
- What are your biggest regrets?

NOW

- What would you do if you knew you had one day, one week, or one month to live? (What person would you praise? What trip would you take? What secret would you tell? What book would you write? What knowledge would you share? What community would you create? What show would you put on?)
- What are your daily worries, what are you scared of, care of the consequence?
- When you think of successful, who is the first person that comes to mind and why?

FUTURE
- What are your 3-year, 5-year, 10-year, 20-year, 30-year dreams?
- List 20 things you would like to do before you die?
- What will be your legacy? (Impact on others, known for when you are gone)

4 - FACE YOUR FEARS

The Premeditation of Evils by Tim Ferriss, Ted Talk. List down your top fears at the moment stopping you from growing to your best self. Start the sentence with, "What if I...lose my parents, quit my job, leave my relationship, jump from a plane, do ayahuasca, travel the world for one year, quit college, start a business, don't pay my debt, etc."

1. DEFINE
   What if I...(list your fear happening)
   Really ask yourself why you are feeling that way to arrive at the bottom core.
   Write 10 worst things that would happen.

2. PREVENT
   How can you prevent these episodes? Or decrease the likelihood of them happening?

3. REPAIR
   Repair. What could I do to repair the damage if my fear happens? Is there anyone else in the history of time who has figured this out? What would be the benefits of an attempt

or partial success? What are the possible good outcomes if you take action?

4. COST OF INACTION
If I avoid these actions, what would my life look like? (Emotionally, physically, financially, etc.)
In six months, in one year, in three years

5. BALANCE YOUR SEVEN WELLNESS LIFE DIMENSIONS
Every 90 days rate, on 1 to 10 without using the number 7, your 7 wellness life dimensions to not have one bad affecting the same way others. When you are not balanced on those 7 wellness life dimensions no matter how hard you work, you'll always end up stuck into a crazy 8 loop over and over again.

PERSONAL (give back/help/social/community)
Score: _____

JOB (daily work, skills, position, domain)
Score: _____

BUSINESS (team/organization/clients/industry)
Score: _____

RELATIONSHIP (family/core friends/spouse & kids)
Score: _____

PHYSICAL (body/health/mental)
Score: _____

FINANCE (cash flow/savings/debt/expenses)
Score: _____

SPIRITUAL (inner-self/love/mindfulness/gratitude)
Score: _____

Choose 1 that you will work intensively in the next 90 days. Which other life dimension it would improve at the same time. WHY.

6. IDENTIFY YOUR PURPOSE WITH THE IKIGAI PHILOSOPHY
    Start with identifying 5–10 answers in your personal and professional life to each of the 4 ikigai quadrant questions above:
    1. What do you LOVE (in your personal and professional life, the contrary of what you hate)?
    2. What are you GOOD AT (that you might like or not like to do)?
    3. What does the WORLD NEED (from your own perspective & vision of the world)?
    4. What can I get PAID FOR (the skills you bring on the table to grow your organization)?

    Then with your answers above, do your quadrant of success:
    5. What you LOVE plus you are good at (PASSION)?
    6. What you don't LOVE plus you are good at (PAYING YOUR BILLS)?
    7. What you LOVE plus are not good at yet (POTENTIAL) (learn more, not yet an expert)?
    8. What you don't LOVE plus are not good at (DAILY TASKS)?

    Finish this exercise with a purpose statement of one sentence. Make it clear that it is your reason to wake up and grow, serve people/world, give back, inspire humans.

    Watch this video of Jay Shetty for in-depth explanations.

7. SET A GRATITUDE STATEMENT AND AFFIRMATIONS

We need a vision to grow, but we need to be grounded, grateful, humble of what we've been through, of our current resources and relationships. Our goal is to live in the now at every situation, moment, second. Act like you'll die tomorrow; grow like you'll live 100 years. Write a 5–10 lines gratitude statement of your life right now.

And why not finishing it with strengthening yourself talks with I AM affirmations. Link them to your Physical, Mental and Emotional self.

I AM _____   _____

8. WRITE A THREE-YEAR LIFE VISION IN THE PRESENT TENSE

From everything you wrote above, write a three-year vision of 1 page (4–5 paragraphs) written in the present tense mentioning your personality, criteria of your relationships, purpose, habits you are proud of, values, virtues, fears faced, experiences you are living, resources you have, type of location, situation, work, business, finance, spirituality, physical dimension, community you are part of, etc..

Then make a vision board and dream book. This is why cavemen drew their dinners on the rocks before hunting. Use canva.com to translate your vision visually with photos, quotes, statements, models, drawing, colors, etc. Carry this visualization tool with you every day or hang it in a place you see it daily. For the moment, put two photos for each of the ideal seven life dimensions vision.

BONUS:

The best way to build your seven wellness life dimensions is to build a community around your personality, purpose, values, vision and passions. Serve yourself as a client of your company; you'll know the market by heart. This could easily become a business if you push hard or it can be turned into a non-profit or it can stay small to satisfy your personal life.

"THE PERSON YOU'LL BE IN 5 YEARS IS BASED ON THE TOP 5 PEOPLE YOU SPEND THE MOST TIME WITH AND THE BOOK YOU READ RIGHT NOW."

Appendix 2

100 PRODUCTIVITY TRICKS THEY WILL NEVER TEACH YOU IN UNIVERSITY

Stop acting like a slave

Since I launched my business in 2011, I always dreamed to live the 4 hours' workweek lifestyle. Reading this book led me to an unstoppable craving for knowledge and skills to master this lifestyle. Year after year, I've been reading books and practicing the art of productivity to get closer to this ideology.

As you probably know by now, the school system is outdated. It will never teach you how to work in the modern age, be efficient and live a healthy balanced life away from mental illness.

We have seven wellness life dimensions. When you are not balanced in those seven wellness life dimensions, no matter how hard you work, you'll always end up stuck into a crazy 8 loop, over and over again.

Rate the following on a scale of 1 (lowest) to 10 (highest) without using the number 7 (ok zone, good enough standard). And then tackle one productivity habit in the dimension you would like to improve in the next 90 days. Chase one rabbit at a time using the Kaizen principle for 66 days straight.

PERSONAL (give back/help/social/community)
Score: _____

JOB (daily work, skills, position, domain)
Score: _____

BUSINESS (colleagues/organization/clients/industry)
Score: _____

RELATIONSHIP (family/core friends/spouse/kids)
Score: _____

PHYSICAL (body/health/mental/stress)
Score: _____

FINANCE (cash flow/savings/debt/expenses/lifestyle)
Score: _____

SPIRITUAL (inner-self/love/mindfulness/gratitude)
Score: _____

PERSONAL

1. **Self-Development Journal:** Journal everyday analyzing your thought process, introspecting your behaviors and emotions, doing exercises, taking notes on what you've learned, listing gratitudes and affirmations. Book: *The 4-Hour Workweek* / Tim Ferriss.
2. **Stack Dominos:** Goal set someday, then 10 years, 5 years and 3 years, and bring it back to year goal, quarter goal, month goal, week goal, and day goal.

3. **Morning Routine:** Prime your brain toward getting into a momentum, put happy vibe music on, drink cold water, do a two-minute long workout yoga or stretching to activate your brain's reactive system, do a five-minute journal affirmation, do positive statements of love and gratitude, 20 minutes body weight, take a cold shower, drink some cold pressed green juice and eat fruits.

4. **The First Ten Minutes of Your Day:** This is a crucial moment when your brain is functioning with the highest amount of brain waves. Everything you hear, think or see will imprint onto your spirit for the rest of your day. Tune in to the right state of mind in the first 10 minutes of your day with mental positive affirmation and a gratitude statement.

5. **Sleep:** You need 7h30–8h a night to get 5 hours of REM Sleep. Try some earplugs, eye cover, and a warm and fluffy blanket. Book: *The sleep revolution* / Arianna Huffington.

6. **Control Your Sleep Thieves:** Don't drink coffee before 12h00, don't eat dinner after 8h30pm, don't use your mind as a memory device, don't watch porn or drama movie/series, don't look at a screen 30 minutes before sleep, etc.

7. **Night Routine:** The goal is to empty your mind and relax your body. Don't eat and check your phone after 21h00, don't plan & set goals for tomorrow after 19h, and don't eat heavy food for dinner on weekdays. Take a hot shower and drink cold water after, and try journaling five minutes about a positive thing that happened that day, then do ten minutes of sleep meditation lying in the bed while doing muscle contractions.

8. **Bed Time:** Go to bed between 8–10pm, around 2h after the sun goes down. Our body is connected with the energy of the sun.

9. **Life-Changing Habits:** Build one life-changing habit at a time for 66 days using the Kaizen principle. We can only

build five life-changing habits a year. If you chase two rabbits at a time, you'll only catch either of them.

10. **Trigger Behaviors:** Set alarms with triggers to act on habits or things you want to improve and then link it to a reward to build the habit loop.

11. **Photo Accountability:** Use Google Photo to track your daily habits, workout, diet, social life, etc.

12. **Stay Settled a Minimum:** 60–90 days in one destination with your steady Airbnb and coworking place in the neighborhood. 20+ minutes of commuting to work can lead to depression.

13. **Dopamine:** Maximize your energy by consuming less dopamine like notifications, drugs, sex, etc.

14. **NOFAP:** No porn, no Tinder, no Instagram. It creates problems with your neurotransmitter because too much dopamine is being released.

15. **Announce Your Goal Publicly:** Write on social media, make a video of what you'll do too. Send it to your friends and post it on all social media sites you subscribe to.

16. **Unconscious Addictions:** Remove them one by one. Things that you do too much without realizing it steal your time for the other seven wellness life dimensions. Ex: burying yourself too much in books.

17. **Affirmation/Self-Talk:** We have a constant conversation running all the time (the Monkey Mind). We have 50k-70k thoughts a day, of which 80% are negative. You need to control all micro negative self-talk and turn them into positive ones.

18. **Learn 60 Minutes Every Day:** 30 minutes in the morning and 30 minutes at night or while commuting. Find your golden nugget of the day and write it down in your journal.

19. **Don't Commute More Than 20 Minutes:** Studies show that people who commute or drive more than 20 minutes to get to work are more depressed.

20. **Consistency:** Five minutes a day is better than 30 minutes three times a week. This is according to the Kaizen principle.

21. **How Are You Living?:** You won an ultra-lottery of being alive, one chance out of 400 trillion where winning the lottery is 1 out of 14 million and getting struck by lightning is 1 out of 10 million, and being killed in a plane crash is 1 out of 11 million.

22. **Visualization:** Create yourself a pocket dream book or board where you hang in your room with images, goals, quotes, models of inspiration, and the things you want.

23. **Your Face Muscles:** Tense forehead muscles with crusty eyes will lead to more stress and less peace. Make sure you are always smiling from the inside with your lips slightly inclined up to attract positive people.

24. **Your Environment:** Your flatmate or house companion is affecting your vibrations. The city or island you live in, and the weather and how comfortable you are also affect your state of mind.

JOB

25. **Willpower:** It's like a phone battery, start the day at 100%. Be aware, manage it and recharge it smartly. These things drain your willpower: implementing new behavior, filtering distractions, resisting temptation, suppressing emotions, restraining aggression, suppressing impulses, taking tests, trying to impress others, coping with fear, doing something you don't like to do, selecting long-term over short-term results, etc. Book: *The willpower Instinct* / Kelly McGonigal.

26. **Your ONE THING**: Every morning for 3–4 hours', work on your one thing that will lead you to extraordinary results. Everything else is a distraction and drains your willpower. Be a maker in the morning; a manager in the afternoon. Book: *The One Thing* / Gary Kelly.

27. **Work from Home:** Work from home in the three hours you woke up to EAT THAT FROG. Book: *Eat That Frog* / Brian Tracy.

28. **Physical Workplace:** Empty and clean your desk, and have a strong back cover. Work with a wall in front of you so you won't be distracted by people passing by. Every three minutes workers get distracted and it takes 11 minutes to get back in focus. Book: *Getting Things Done* / David Allen.

29. **Wi-Fi & Desk:** Chase 20mbps or more Wi-Fi. A good workplace, carry a pocket Wi-Fi, get an unlimited sim card. Work from a steady desk with a chair with a good back cover.

30. **The 80/20 Pareto Law:** It states that roughly 80% of the effects come from 20% of the causes. Analyze every detail of your life and work with it to focus on what matters.

31. **Pomodoro Technique:** Do a minimum of 8 blocks of 25 minutes per day. Your brain can only work with a focus of 90 minutes at a time with a peak of concentration at 45 minutes.

32. **Multitasking:** Never ever multitask; it's the most toxic thing for your productivity. You lose 20% of your time in a day. Having two windows open on your computer at the same time is a form of multitasking.

33. **Track Everything:** Track your work with Toggl/Desktime/Hubstaff and do your finances weekly with Mint, and go over your goals with an accountability partner.

34. **Flow/Deep Work:** Your ideal massive goal is to train yourself to go into flow/deep work every day. Book: *Deep Work: Rules for Focused Success in a Distracted World* / Cal Newport;

FLOW: The Psychology of optimal experience / Mihaly Csikszentmihalyi.

35. **432hz Music:** Listen to it while working or going to sleep (classic, guitar, instrumental, movie trailer). If you are working and listening to music with lyrics, you are multitasking because your subconscious tries to process those words even if you don't understand the language.

36. **Emails Are Toxic:** Master the email game to do email 3h/week. Filtering, labeling, using two addresses, autoresponder and don't show the email Google Chrome extension and block site extensions in the morning and at night.

37. **Accountability Partner:** Find an accountability partner or Coach and log in daily and track your evolution. HabitBull mobile app.

38. **Motivation is garbage:** Trick your brain to act within *the 5 Second Rule*. Tedtalk: How to Stop Screwing Yourself Over | Mel Robbins.

39. **Be Agile:** Constantly analyze your time at hand with your resources and willpower level to see if a five minutes' specific task could be done.

40. **Success Brings More Success:** Reach the momentum principle of success.

41. **Finish It Now:** Finish the task at hand now to not lose 500% of your time.

42. **Tomorrow Goal Planning:** Plan tomorrow today before quitting work. It's only ten minutes of your work session.

43. **Give Up Perfection:** Launch publicly at 80% done, put your ego aside and ask for feedback from your targeted audience.

44. **No Watch Day:** Battle manic-depression with worry breaks with no watch

45. **Worries Are an Illusion:** Worries = stress = burnout = depression = hard to do anything productive.

46. **Your #1 Professional Skill:** Master and improve it constantly. This is what you are paid for. When you work with it, you bring the greatest value to your organization. The average CEO works 28 minutes a day on it. Book: *The Compound Effect* / Darren Hardy.

47. **You're Being Paid to Rest:** Maximize sleep and off times, play time, hobbies, social life, and stabilize your seven wellness life dimensions. Don't work to go on vacation, live in vacation and take breaks going to work. Plan your vacation calendar for the next 12 months with 2 months' of work sessions in between.

48. **Improve One Skill at a Time:** There's too much knowledge and information out there. Every four months, focus on one skill by learning and acting on the top books, Ted talks, podcasts, and YouTube tutorials.

49. **Emergency Channel:** Set up one that only a vital few know about. Use different chat apps with notifications that you use with those rare people.

BUSINESS

50. **Start With Why:** List 20 reasons why you will never give up. Book/Ted Talk: Start With Why / Simon Sinek.

51. **Leaders Eat Last:** Let other people express their opinion first; it will help their sense of involvement without affecting their perspective and allow you to have the perspective of everyone before you express your opinion. Book/Ted Talk: *Leaders Eat Last* / Simon Sinek.

52. **Voice vs Typing:** Send voice messages (220 words/minute) instead of writing (70 words/minute). 80% of the web will be audio and video by 2020, now 30% of Google searches are made by voice.

53. **Record Screencast:** Make a mini video training recording your screen while talking to show exactly one thing to get done right instead of planning a meeting for it. Use the Loom extension.

54. **Hire Slowly and Fire Quickly:** You are better off finding someone fitting your values and your company's culture than one having the best CV. Enthusiasm and commitment are better than skills. A badly managed employee will end up costing you four times his salary over a period of 12 months.

55. **Written/Text Message:** Never ever bring up concerns via text message. Message only to give respect to humans.

56. **Set Up All Expectations:** For all coworkers, clients, suppliers with clear announcement automation.

PHYSICAL

57. **Drink Water:** Get water and prepare to not have to break your flow, at least two liters per day of filtered water. Don't trust the corporation selling you bad water. Carry your water in a blue bottle with crystal at the bottom.

58. **Exercise:** 20 minutes minimum daily to re-oxygenate your mind.

59. **What the Health:** Eat on your own self-aware terms. Food is your carburetor. If after eating you don't feel more energized, you didn't eat real food or you ate too much. Eat for 20 minutes and until you feel you are 80% full.

60. **Stress/Fears/Doubt-Free:** Stress is the biggest killer of dreams. When you are stressed, you can't think, you can't work, and you can't have energy.

61. **Fasting:** Water fasting for three days for 2–3 times a year can give you 20 years of longevity. Read in depth about it, and make sure to break your fast properly.

62. **Coffee Enema:** All diseases come from the gut. Clean your colon with the German technique recommended from the cancer research institute.
63. **Not eating badly treated animals:** When you eat dead animals that were badly beaten up, and raised with no care, you eat their attitude, stress, and suffering. Stop eating any kind of meat for 10 days, then eat it for only a day and you'll see the devastating realization on your thought patterns.
64. **Regulate Legal Drugs:** Salt, refined sugar, caffeine, alcohol, nicotine. All those should be consumed as less as possible to keep a balanced mind.

FINANCE

65. **5% Love Account:** Collect a little bit weekly and always give it in person quarterly to an initiative that you really care about. And you need to see in person the people benefiting from it. *Book: Give and Take* / Adam Grant.
66. **Pay Yourself First:** Pay yourself 10% of your monthly income before all other monthly bills. Put the 10% pay in an investment account. Book: *The Richest Man in Babylon* / George Clason.
67. **Outsourcing:** Outsource all your handy tasks in the Philippines, India, Easter Europe, Colombia, and Venezuela.
68. **Personal Assistant:** Use one to buy, search, book, schedule, remind, and contact. Upwork.com.
69. **Weekly Finance Report:** Take 30 minutes to analyze and give feedback each Sunday. MINT App.
70. **Invest Your Savings:** Every quarter or semester, invest your $5,000 and pay yourself first by putting your savings into a project linked to your resources.

RELATIONSHIP

71. **Find Mentors:** Seek advice from people who have achieved 10% more than you did.

72. **Masterminds:** Gather 2–3 friends into a weekly one-hour Mastermind to build on things you have learned and support each other.

73. **Build Your Community:** It's the most fulfilling way to satisfy your social life and the best way to start a business.

74. **Become a Massive LOVER:** Hug everyone you care about with your head on the right side to have a heart-to-heart connection.

75. **Say No Gracefully:** When you know where you are going, it is easy to see what can help you get to your destination or not. From that point, you'll hardly have to say no to very many opportunities.

76. **Everyone Is Insecure:** At every level people don't know what they are doing. Everyone is trying to figure it out. So don't care about what other people think.

77. **Praising Someone:** Send out 3–4 minutes personal video messages praising someone for their support or work and it will give you a massive energy burst.

78. **Your Top Five:** The person you'll be in five years is based on the five people you hang out with the most and the books you read today. Make a life audit to spend more time with your top five.

SPIRITUAL

79. **Minimalist Lifestyle:** Stop worrying for stuff to free up your mind's bandwidth.

80. **Meditate Daily:** To control your mind's wandering and processing negative thoughts.

81. **Seven Wellness Life Dimensions:** Satisfy your seven dimensions one at a time choosing the one that can affect the other at the same time. These are finance, spiritual, personal, job, business, relationship, and physical.

82. **Power of Now:** It's the only thing that is real. Books: *The Power of Now* / Eckhart Tolle; *The Compass of Now* / DDnard, *Be Here now* / Ram Dass.

83. **Be a Teacher:** Teaching is the end of the circle of learning. There's always someone in your entourage to inspire, mentor, and support mentally.

84. **Find Your Temple:** The gym, meditation room, library/bookstore. We all need these places to go evacuate our worries and doubts when things get dark.

85. **100% Responsible:** We are the problem and the solution all at the same time.

86. **Creative Procrastination:** There's always one thing we love that we do too much.

87. **We Are All Procrastinators:** Know when to stop it, and break the cycle. Set a daily due date. Tedtalk: Inside the Mind of a Master Procrastinator | Tim Urban.

88. **True Wealth:** Don't chase recognition, trophies, money, or fame. Real success is about how many people you were able to serve today, and how many you've impacted. Start small with your sister/brother, and parents. It will make you fly.

89. **Don't Be a Copycat:** Take a bit of what you like from everybody.

90. **Listen Mindfully:** Humans can talk on average 220 words a minute, but can process only 550 a minute, and that's why your mind wanders when you listen to someone or listen with the intent of responding. Listening mindfully creates deep human connections.

91. **Control Your Decisions**: Disable all notifications, and put Adblock on your laptop and Browser AdBlock on your phone, download music on your phone instead of YouTube or Spotify with ads. The goal is to find ways that you hear about them eight times. Show your phone who is the boss of your life.

92. **Write Everything Down on Paper:** Cognitive reaction and it frees up your mind. You want to do everything you can to not use your mind as a memory device.

93. **Self-Talk:** Control your self-talk so as to be constantly optimistic and positive. Micro negative self-talk is a soul killer.

94. **Change Your words, Change Your Life:** Stop saying 'I don't have time', or 'I am too busy'. Make the time. We always have time to do what we like. Stop saying 'I can't afford that', and make a plan to afford it.

95. **Your Major Key Constraints:** Empty your bag of rocks. What is holding you back? What past wounds are you still carrying in your day-to-day life?

96. **Weapons of Mass Distraction**: Remove the temptation and track your behavior using Block App, Rescue Time, News Feed Eradicator, and Plane Mode.

97. **Clean Up Virtual Space:** Google Drive, Favoris, hard drive, and Social Accounts, to free up your mind and feel lighter.

98. **Deconstruct Your Ego:** *Ego Is the Enemy* / Ryan Holiday, if it is too big, it will lead you to a dangerous path that will always backfire on you. Live an immersive spiritual experience of more than 10 days to start the deconstruction.

99. **Access the Spiritual Dimension:** An Ayahuasca retreat or smoking DMT will lead you to comprehend your deepest demons, your most oppressive thoughts, the spiritual dimension, and even experience death.

100. **The Dharma Lifestyle:** Make a ten-day vipassana silent meditation retreat to learn this unique 2,500-year-old technique to access the universe inside you.

Appendix 3

20 QUOTES INSPIRING
YOU TO BE YOUR HIGHER SELF

"If you look at what you have in life, you'll always have more. If you look at what you don't have in life, you'll never have enough."
~ Oprah Winfrey

"Our truest life is when we are in dreams awake."
~ Henry David Thoreau

"Nothing is impossible; the word itself says 'I'm possible'!"
~ Audrey Hepburn

"Someday, somewhere, anywhere, unfailingly,
you'll find yourself, and that, and only that,
can be the happiest or bitterest hour of your life."
~ Pablo Neruda

"Each man's life represents a road toward himself."
~ Hermann Hesse

"Lose yourself wholly;
and the more you lose, the more you will find."
~ Catherine Of Siena

"Knowing yourself is the beginning of all wisdom."
~ Aristotle

"People often say that this or that person has not yet
found himself. But the self is not something one finds,
it is something one creates."
~ Thomas Szasz

"All the wonders you seek are within yourself."
~ Thomas Browne

"Life is either a daring adventure or nothing at all."
~ Helen Keller

"The journey not the arrival matters."
~ T.S. Eliot

"Jobs fill your pocket, but adventures fill your soul."
~ Jamie Lyn Beatty

"If you're twenty-two, physically fit, hungry to learn and be
better, I urge you to travel—as far and as widely as possible.
Sleep on floors if you have to. Find out how other people live
and eat and cook. Learn from them—wherever you go."
~ Anthony Bourdain

"Traveling—it leaves you speechless,
then turns you into a storyteller."
~ Ibn Battuta

"Travel is the only thing you buy that makes you richer."
~ Anonymous

"Collect Moment, Not Things."
~ Anonymous

"Travel far enough, you meet yourself."
~ David Mitchell

"A journey of a thousand miles begins with a single step"
~ Lao Tzu

"Travel doesn't become adventure until you leave yourself behind"
~ Marty Rubin

"A good traveler has no fixed plans, and is not intent on arriving."
~ Lao Tzu

"A journey is best measured in friends rather than miles."
~ Tim Cahill

Appendix 4

TOP TEN BOOKS TO READ TO
START YOUR JOURNEY TOWARD MASTERY

- *Think and Grow Rich* by Napoleon Hill
- *The 4-Hour Workweek* by Tim Ferriss
- *The One Thing* by Gary Keller
- *The Power of Now* by Eckhart Tolle
- *How to Win Friends and Influence People* by Dale Carnegie
- *Rich Dad Poor Dad* by Robert Kiyosaki
- *Start with Why* by Simon Sinek
- *The Untethered Soul* by Michael Singer
- *Dotcom Secrets* by Russell Brunson
- *The Little Red Book of Selling* by Jeffrey Gitomer

Appendix 5

ERASMUS STUDENTS
SHARING THEIR STORIES AND INSIGHTS

YOUTUBE VIDEOS

Leaving + Arriving | Copenhagen Study Abroad
https://www.youtube.com/watch?v=4NAViQQdUdk

Arriving in Europe + French Room Tour | Study Abroad
https://www.youtube.com/watch?v=pJhYc76KoZU

Post-Erasmus Depression Syndrome
https://www.youtube.com/watch?v=S5qdR2ssi7I

The Erasmus Depression - TES #28
https://www.youtube.com/watch?v=CJaawZmDIDM&

Things to Know Before Your Erasmus Year Abroad
https://www.youtube.com/watch?v=8zOqxfGSNk0&

Eight Top Tips for Surviving Culture shock
https://www.youtube.com/watch?v=EpJJ2f0FWpM

CULTURE SHOCK -- je suis en france! (French Study Abroad Vlog #11)
https://www.youtube.com/watch?v=d0GNp_89CLk

ARTICLES

Article of a student releasing all her emotions on paper after exchange:
https://medium.com/@marinabozhenko/life-after-erasmus-4c0cacb099ff

Article of an exchange student talking about her experience one year later:
https://medium.com/@ciuca.ioanacristina/why-erasmus-isnt-just-about-partying-9ff98ba6498d

Ten Tips for Studying Abroad in 2019
https://medium.com/@arrvl/10-tips-for-studying-abroad-in-2019-4e0c78e8005

Three surprising ways I made my Erasmus more organized and fun
https://medium.com/@pCloud/3-surprising-ways-i-made-my-eramsus-more-organized-and-fun-35283e366fc8

Ten things I wished I'd known before moving to England
https://medium.com/writing-in-the-media/10-things-i-wished-id-known-before-moving-to-england-e632c926c586

Erasmus : Amortir le choc des cultures
https://medium.com/@camilleelaraki/erasmus-amortir-le-choc-des-cultures-c0f58784f318